The 21ˢᵗ Century Agent

THE
STRATEGIC
COACH®

The 21st Century Agent

Dan Sullivan

The Strategic Coach®, Strategic Coach®, The Strategic Coach Program™, The Great
Crossover™, Free Days™, Focus Days™, Buffer Days™, The Entrepreneurial Time
System™, The Ceiling Of Complexity™, The Six Laws Of The Microchip™, Global
Status System™, and The 21st Century Agent™ are trademarks of The Strategic
Coach Inc.

Printed in Toronto, Canada. The Strategic Coach Inc., 33 Fraser Avenue, Suite 201,
Toronto, Ontario M6K 3J9. This book was designed and typeset on a Macintosh
computer by Sonja Moser. The Cover graphic was created by Sean Tamblyn.

This publication is meant to strengthen your common sense, not to substitute for
it. It is also not a substitute for the advice of your doctor, lawyer, accountant, or any
of your advisors, personal or professional.

FIRST EDITION

Canadian Cataloguing in Publication Data

Sullivan Dan, 1944 -
The 21st Century Agent

ISBN 0-9698401-3-6 (book)
ISBN 0-9698401-4-4 (set of 8 audiotapes)
ISBN 0-9698401-2-8 (book and audiotapes)

1. Insurance, Life.   2. Life insurance agents.
I. Title

HG8771.S85 1995   368.3'2   C95-931591-8

**If you would like further information about The Strategic Coach
Program™, and other Strategic Coach® services and products, please
telephone 416-531-7399 or 1-800-387-3206.**

Welcome To The 21st Century Agent!

This book also has a companion set of seven hours of audio recordings on eight cassettes. Either reading the book or listening to the audio tapes will be of benefit. However, they are complementary and I encourage you to also listen to the audio tapes in order to receive the greatest impact.

Table Of Contents

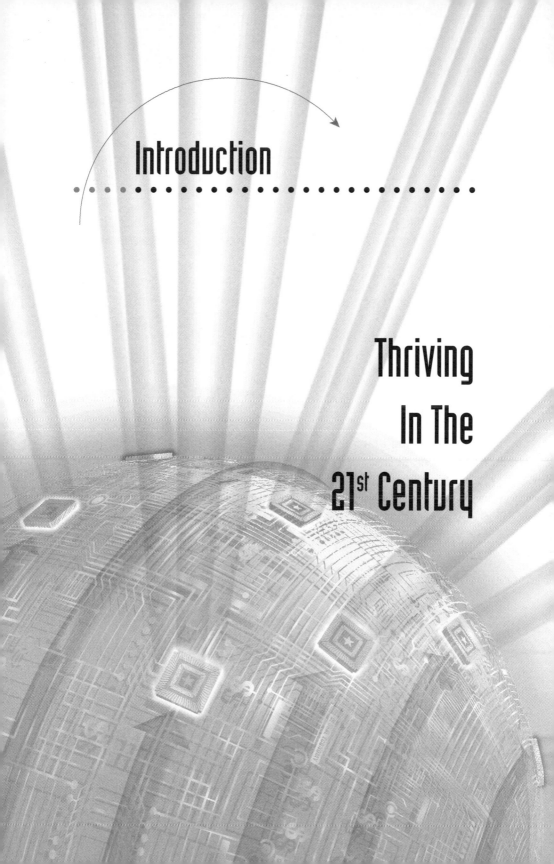

Introduction

Thriving In The 21st Century

Introduction

In the spring of 1992, I was invited to address some of the head office personnel of a large life insurance company, and I started my speech in the following manner:

"I understand there are 500 of you sitting in this audience. I just want you to know that if they invite me back in 2002, there are going to be only 50 people sitting here. Isn't that great? That means that the other 450 of you will get a chance to do something else with your lives."

Needless to say, the response was less than enthusiastic. One man, a director-level executive, took me aside afterwards:

"That's not possible! You have to understand that we've already gone through a tremendous downsizing. We're as lean as we can be."

My response was that if I had erred in my prediction, it was probably on the conservative side. A year later, I learned that 125 personnel, including the executive who had talked to me, had been "downsized."

I tell this story to emphasize the general environment in which life insurance agents are going to be working over the next 25 years.

Insurance companies at the turn of the 21ˢᵗ century, even the most successful companies, will have no choice except to become much smaller, more efficient organizations. Global forces, more powerful than the insurance industry itself, are causing a reorganization of all economic relationships on the planet.

Insurance companies, in response to these forces, will strive to cut costs wherever they can, primarily by substituting technology for people.

This transformation is already having a profound impact on the status and security of life insurance agents, and many individuals, unable to adjust to the changes, may not survive the upheavals that lie ahead.

This book is meant to provide a 25 year framework, both conceptual and strategic, for surviving and thriving as a life insurance agent at the outset of the 21ˢᵗ century.

But, first, exactly what is a "21ˢᵗ Century Agent"?

Put simply, he or she is *an entrepreneur with a specialty in life insurance* who has adopted a set of concepts and strategies that are, in many respects, diametrically opposed to those which have been taught and learned within the career agency systems of most insurance companies since the middle of the 19ᵗʰ century.

Specifically, The 21ˢᵗ Century Agent is someone who:

• *Recognizes that ongoing changes in the life insurance industry are beyond his or her personal control and, for the most part, are beyond the control of the industry itself.*

We are living in an age of global economic upheaval during which the entire structure of the life insurance industry — especially relationships between companies and agents — is already being transformed in fundamental ways.

Introduction

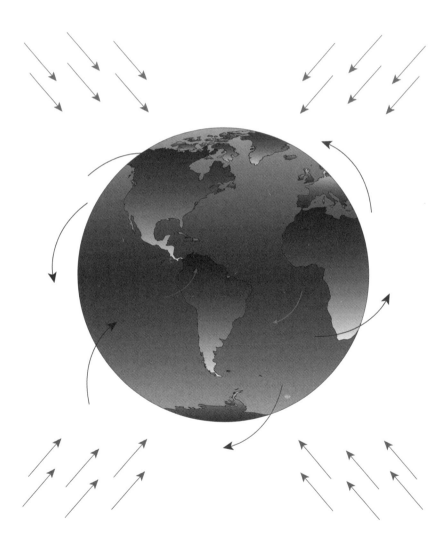

• Identifies and utilizes the major forces that are transforming the global economy and the life insurance industry.

He or she focuses on taking advantage of these forces, regardless of what the insurance companies do. This means taking an entrepreneurial approach to every aspect of the insurance practice. This, in turn, means eliminating the sense of employee-like dependency on company decision making and strategies that still characterize the thinking of most agents in the 1990s.

• Takes total responsibility for his or her success as a life insurance agent.

The primary relationship of life agents is no longer with an insurance company or with the insurance industry but with individual consumers in the global economic system. The design of effective insurance products and services is now dictated by the demands of millions of consumers who feel unprotected by the institutions of their national societies. Life insurance consumers at the end of the 20ᵗʰ century feel no loyalty to any company but seek, instead, the knowledge and skill of individual economic agents who are able to operate as independent counselors and problem solvers.

• Thinks ahead 25 years and describes how he or she wants to do business at that point — then uses this vision as a guide for immediate decisions and actions.

Twenty-first Century Agents will build their businesses around 25-year goals that are oblivious to existing insurance company priorities, policies, and contracts. The successful insurance practice over the next quarter century will be based on an agent's personal alignment with the emerging rules of the global economic system — especially those related to the evolution of microtechnology.

• Creates a business future that is autonomous of the career survival of head office bureaucrats.

It becomes increasingly necessary for agents to insulate themselves from the organizational fallout caused by the restructuring of insurance head offices as they grapple with global change. As we move through the 1990s, more bureaucratic jobs will disappear as insurance companies consolidate and merge, or go bankrupt. Much of the job loss will occur in the senior ranks and among career agency management.

Those job positions which survive within substantially smaller organizations will require radically different knowledge, skills, and attitudes.

No insurance agent who chooses to succeed as an entrepreneur over the next 25 years can afford to tie his or her future prospects to those of individuals in the industry who have chosen not to be entrepreneurs.

• *Finally, The 21ˢᵗ Century Agent is someone who masters entrepreneurial strategies that will remain valid regardless of what changes take place within the insurance industry over the next 25 years.*

These strategies, which are explained in the second part of this book, are ways of thinking, planning, and acting that turn all negative trends within the industry into opportunities.

But they are more than that! Taken together, the 20 strategies, when mastered, provide a new structure that eliminates all bureaucratic dependencies over an entire lifetime.

Creating an insurance policy for your life insurance career.

Earlier this century, author Franz Kafka wrote: "In any conflict between yourself and the world, back the world."

Right now, the "world," in the form of global economic changes, is telling every life insurance agent to become a *total entrepreneur*. Many agents will not heed the challenge and will find themselves burdened with head office dependencies and sucked into a vortex of bureaucratic crises, complexities, complications, and confusions.

Many other agents, however, are already making the "entrepreneurial leap" by following the course outlined in the following pages.

They are creating a lifetime insurance policy for their life insurance careers by becoming fully knowledgeable about the 21st century trends affecting their futures and by mastering the strategies that will enable them to be 21st Century Agents.

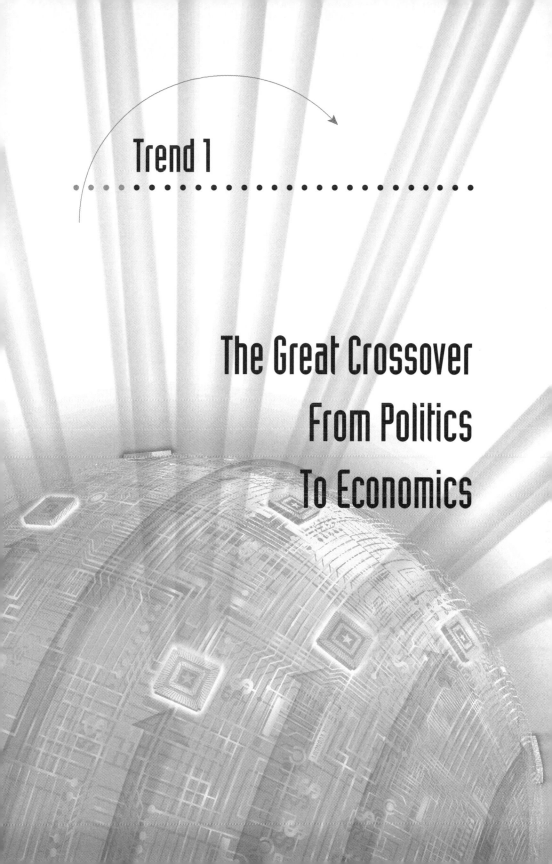

Trend 1

The Great Crossover
From Politics
To Economics

Trend 1

• •

Since approximately 1970, all of global society has been to some degree in the process of making a "great crossover" — from a world based primarily on politics to one where the primary organizing structure is economics. For the next 50 to a 100 years we will see two dominant phenomena in the world:

One, the growth of global economic systems and networks based on the principle of unlimited entrepreneurial expansion.

Two, the diminishing, disintegration, and collapse of national governments based on the principle of bureaucratic control, regulation, and intervention.

This great crossover — the transition from politics to economics, the transition from bureaucracy to entrepreneurism — has two primary causes: one that is apparent to nearly everyone and another that is largely hidden.

Most people will come to see *the rise of global consumerism* as the force that is changing the nature of economic growth, political management, social welfare, and cultural development in all countries.

The endless creation of new products and services, and the expansion of vast consumer and capital markets across national borders will increasingly weaken the hold that central governments of nation states have on the aspirations and activities of their citizens. This is either a wonderful or a terrible development, depending on one's perspective, resources, abilities, and ambitions.

For many people, whose hopes and dreams are based on entrepreneurial risk-taking, this will be a wonderful time to be alive. It will be the greatest period of entrepreneurial opportunity in history. It will be a time filled with excitement, creativity, success, and satisfaction.

For many others, whose security has been dependent upon cradle-to-grave bureaucratic protection, the new world of global consumerism will seem frightening. Decreases in bureaucratic security will seem like a betrayal of fundamental ideals, values and promises. It will seem to many men and women who have known only bureaucratic education and employment that their most cherished traditions and beliefs are being attacked.

Above all, the opportunities and rewards of this new world will seem terribly unequal and unjust to the bureaucratic mentality. For those individuals who have become habituated to the comforts, perks, subsidies, grants, entitlements, guarantees, and the so-called equality of the modern welfare state, the future will look bleak, if not catastrophic.

In short, for all of those who have come to see modern civilization as necessarily based on massive, centralized government — and on large bureaucratic institutions in all other sectors of society — the growth of global consumerism will seem like the decline of everything that is desirable, beneficial, and precious.

But for all its undeniable impact, whether viewed positively or negatively, consumerism is only a surface explanation for the extraordinary changes taking place in global society. There is another factor — something deeper, more fundamental, more disruptive and transforma-

Trend 1

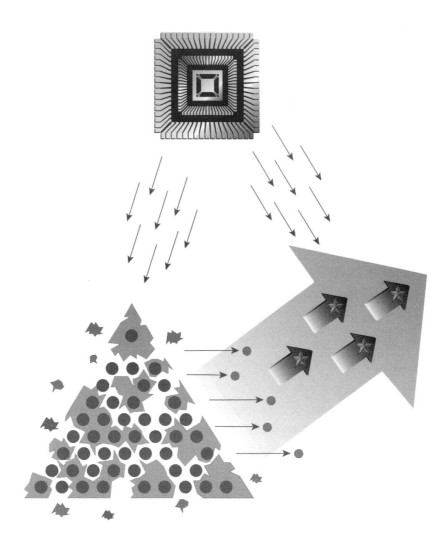

tive — that is the cause of consumerism and virtually all other economic, political, social, and cultural changes that will take place over the next century:

Microtechnology.

The primary force of change in the world is the never-ending improvement of the microchip, a tiny device for processing and transmitting all kinds of information at an incomprehensible rate of speed. The evolution of the microchip, and its rapid dissemination throughout the world over the past quarter century, has undermined the power and status of political authorities in every society without most people being aware of how or when this occurred.

Before the microchip, virtually all economic relationships were subject to political control. The flow of capital, in particular, could be regulated tightly within national borders, and therefore most industries and forms of employment could be protected, expanded, limited, or even prevented through political intervention.

Politicians and government bureaucrats were the acknowledged powerbrokers in the pre-microchip world, and this had been the case since the 15ᵗʰ century when Gutenburg invented movable type. The introduction of mass printing had created the conditions of centrally-controlled communications necessary for the bureaucratic operation and expansion of national governments.

But all the control that the printing press gave to government bureaucracies over five long centuries, the microchip has taken away in 25 short years.

Because of microchip-based communication networks, the flow of capital has been liberated across national borders. It has escaped from national political control to such a degree that it is now the global capital markets that dictate policy and performance to national politicians and bureaucrats.

At the end of the 20th century, the power of the political elite over economic activities — even their comprehension of economic matters — is eroding quickly in every country, almost on a daily basis.

It is now members of the entire class of economic agents, and this includes life insurance agents, who are the power brokers in modern societies, and this will be increasingly true throughout the 21st century.

Not all economic agents will be successful in this great crossover from politics to economics; *only those who operate as entrepreneurs and who use microtechnology to their competitive advantage will succeed.*

For at least the past 60 years, governments in all countries have taken increasing responsibility for the economic welfare of individuals and groups. This period of global socialism is ending quickly. We are now witnessing a massive movement everywhere — forced by the impact of microtechnology — to privatize much of what has been publicly funded, regulated, and managed in all sectors of society.

This is where the role of the economic agent, especially in the life insurance industry, will become crucial in society over the next 25 years and throughout the next century, namely:

* *Assistance:*

To assist some of the billions of individuals who can no longer depend on government for economic guidance and security.

* *Expertise:*

To become an expert on economic needs and choices, especially of those other successful entrepreneurs who will be creating the majority of wealth-creation and employment opportunities in a decentralized world.

* *Education:*

To become teachers of entrepreneurial principles to clients, customers, suppliers, employees, and family members.

• *Leadership:*

To become a leader in the rejuvenation of community environments and resources in every locale, based on an entrepreneurial rather than a bureaucratic approach to the future.

• *Inspiration:*

And, to become a role model for many others, demonstrating through one's professional autonomy, achievement, and personal quality of life that the age of bureaucratic dependency which has dominated modern societies for most of the 20ᵗʰ century need not continue into the 21ˢᵗ.

One hundred years from now, people will study the 50 years from 1970 to 2020 as one of the three or four greatest periods of historical change, when everything that people thought, said, and did reflected an entirely new perspective. Like all times of great change, this period will not be peaceful, orderly, or satisfying for the majority of people living through it. Most will find it stressful; many will find it threatening. There will be a great market for nostalgia in all areas of life, as people wish for and crave the simplicities of some imagined past. Others will become so frightened that they will resort to fundamentalist strategies that involve rigid systems of belief and behavior.

But while all these negative factors and reactions are making the headlines, there will be a steady growth of individuals and groups who are attuned to the new world that is taking form amidst the wreckage of the old. These are the 21ˢᵗ century people, in every field of human activity, who have let go of the past, who do not wish for its return, and who are focused on making the best of an entirely new situation.

Among this growing population of forward-looking individuals will be The 21ˢᵗ Century Agents™.

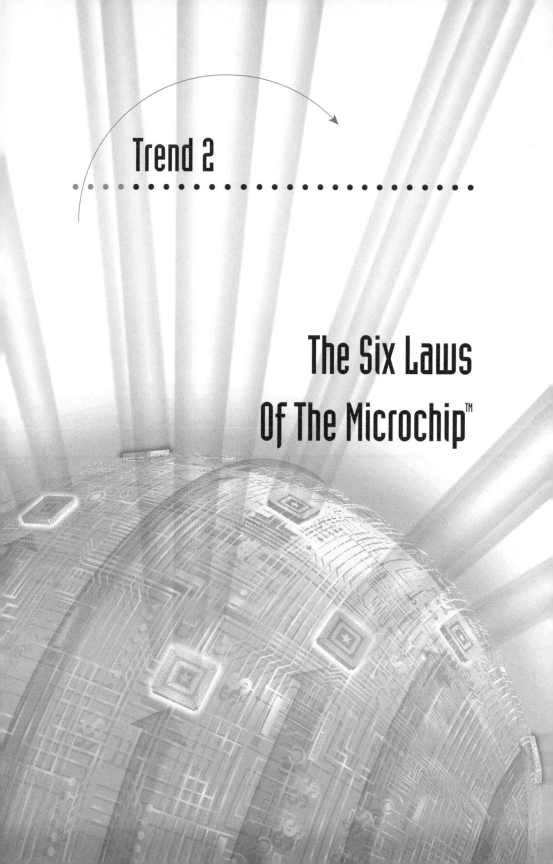

Trend 2

The Six Laws
Of The Microchip™

Trend 2

The utilization of microtechnology over the past quarter century has already created a radically new approach to economic organization on the planet. In the process, virtually all traditional concepts of leadership within government, business, academia, religion, the community, and the family, have been called into question.

But the traditional leadership classes of most countries are resisting this new reality. For the most part, they are still attempting to organize human knowledge and skills, produce products and services, and create revenues and wealth as if the microchip had not been invented.

In particular, millions of individuals in all economic sectors — including the life insurance industry — are attempting to avoid entering into the new economic world by clinging to an outmoded concept of organization, *bureaucracy,* and an outmoded concept of work and compensation, where individuals are paid for *time and effort rather than results.*

Although equipment and systems based on microtechnology have been widely adapted, especially in the English-speaking world, the thought processes of many executives, managers, and workers are still entrenched in the age of bureaucracy. They have failed to understand (or do not want to admit) that microtechnology is not just a new kind of tool, not just a more efficient way to process work, and not just a faster way to communicate.

Rather, microtechnology is an entire value system and philosophy of life that challenges directly most of the principles and practices that have been the foundation of bureaucratic society throughout the 20ᵗʰ century. Microtechnology does not make bureaucracies more efficient; microtechnology destroys bureaucracies. We are not witnessing the transformation of bureaucratic civilization into a more effective stage but the end of that civilization and of all the systems of education, power, status, and security that have grown up around it for more than 100 years.

Like all previous value systems, the new economic world of the microchip is based on certain evolving laws which, during the 21ˢᵗ century, will force the re-evaluation of all economic, political, social, and cultural relationships in global society.

There are six laws in particular that can be articulated at this point:

Microchip Law 1:

The speed of microchips doubles every 18 months.

This phenomenon is widely referred to as Moore's law, after Gordon Moore, who, along with Robert Noyce, developed the first microchip in 1958. In 1965, after observing how the microchip developed, Mr. Moore predicted that it would continue to double its productive capabilities every 18 months, and for the past 30 years his forecast has been remarkably accurate. In fact, microchip manufacturers now plan their new products on this schedule.

Trend 2

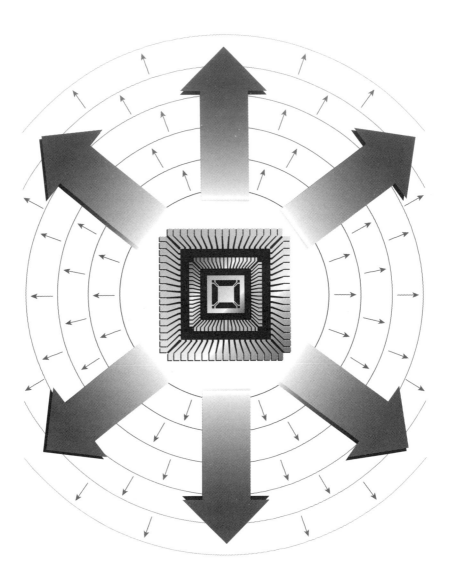

Law 1 says that productivity in human organizations will no longer increase at an incremental rate, a little bit at a time over long periods, but rather at an *exponential rate* — huge increases of performance and results on a frequent basis.

Never before have human beings had to deal with a force of change that continually and unpredictably disrupts, alters, and transforms everything in their environment at an exponential rate. Bureaucratic structures in particular, with their cumbersome hierarchies of command, rigid job descriptions, and conformity-based reward systems, are incapable of responding creatively to a technology that can double productivity every year-and-a-half.

Microchip Law 2:

The microchip favors individuals over organizations.

Bureaucracies have been with us for a long time and have become massive and powerful for a simple reason. Prior to the introduction of microtechnology, human beings had no better way to deal with the complexities of modern life.

Individuals needed the capital, resources, reputation, expertise, decision making, training, efficiency, and sanction of bureaucratic structures in order to live comfortably and work productively in societies with millions of other individuals. Until very recently, it made very good sense for most individuals to secure lifetime employment within large bureaucratic organizations. It was safe. It was comfortable. It was predictable. There was status attached to it. And if you were bureaucratically talented, there was constant opportunity for promotion.

All of that has now changed because the microchip makes it possible for the most ambitious, talented, resourceful individuals in every society to succeed and prosper outside of bureaucracy.

Single individuals and small groups supported by microchip-based tools, systems, and networks, can now out-think, out-create, out-produce, out-maneuver, and out-compete large institutions with thousands of bureaucratic employees. Investment costs for new technology have plummeted to a few thousand dollars, and now only the creativity and skill of a single person, or a small team of similarly motivated individuals, is required to create profitable new businesses and industries.

Each new generation of "twice-as-fast microchips" is utilized more quickly and creatively by enterprising individuals than by less-motivated bureaucratic workers within large institutions.

Microchip Law 3:

Cheaper information always drives out expensive information.

Continual advances in microtechnology — in both hardware and software — now make it possible to collect, organize, store, transform, package, and distribute vast amounts of information at a fraction of the cost possible even two years ago.

This is another reason why bureaucracies are failing fast.

One way of looking at it is that bureaucracies are just rudimentary, "dinosaur" forms of microchips, with human beings serving as the transistors. Prior to the availability of microchip-based equipment and systems, the most important processors of information in society were bureaucratic organizations.

In fact, thousands of individuals are still employed by government, corporations, and other large institutions to keep track of things. Most job descriptions in these organizations involve little more than moving information from one place to another, adding significant cost and not much value in the process. All in all, this makes for very expensive information by the time it is actually used, either inside or outside of the bureaucracy.

Most of these bureaucratic job functions are now replaceable, In whole or part, by software programs that are significantly cheaper, faster, more adaptable, and easier to improve upon than the human individuals who now hold the jobs. As microtechnology continues to improve at an exponential rate, the elimination of bureaucratic employment will keep pace.

Cheaper (microchip) information always drives out expensive (bureaucratic) information.

Microchip Law 4:

Innovation is now cheaper than competition.

As we approach the 21st century, virtually all business — even manufacturing, resources, retail, and agriculture — is involved with the "knowledge economy." This is particularly true of all service businesses, which represent the fastest growing sector in the global economy.

In the knowledge economy, the greatest marketing breakthroughs and financial gains are achieved through the innovation of new products and services rather than through head-to-head competition over existing products or services.

The economist Paul Zane Pilzer says that wealth creation in all sectors of the global economy now follows a formula:

$$W = R \times T$$
$$\text{Wealth} = \text{Resources} \times \text{Technology}$$

Resources in this regard can be anything: iron ore, people, money, inventory, real estate, relationships, raw data — anything whose existing value in the marketplace can be multiplied by the application of new techniques, methods, or processes. Each time this formula is triggered, an innovation emerges, and with each *successful* new innovation there also emerges, for a period of time, a unique market niche where profit margins are high because there is no competition. Sony Corporation, for example, introduces an average of one new product every 24 hours.

The best economic opportunities for individuals in the 21st century — in some cases, *the only economic opportunities* — will be for creative "knowledge workers," individuals who specialize in adding new value (innovations) to existing products and services.

Microchip Law 5:

The microchip disconnects money from time and effort.

The basic measuring stick for personal value within the bureaucratic world for more than a century has been the "work hour": the number of hours that bureaucratic employees devoted to their jobs. Within this value system, those who worked long hours were considered more valuable and praiseworthy than those who didn't — *irrespective of the results that were produced outside the bureaucracy.*

This work-hour attitude measurement of value, however, is quickly coming to an end as the impact of microtechnology on all economic sectors radically changes our understanding of productivity.

In the microchip-based economy of the 21st century, the amount of time and effort devoted to a job will be largely irrelevant. In fact, the very concept of a "job" is losing its meaning as work becomes increasingly "results-based" — geared to opportunities, projects, and special situations where extraordinary financial results are possible if one achieves the best results.

The question of getting paid in the marketplace no longer relates to the amount of time and effort put in but rather to what results are achieved.

Using Pilzer's formula from Law 4, Wealth = Resources x Technology, the resource called "worker" is now disconnected from time and effort on the job, and permanently connected to the constant evolution of the microchip. An individual's economic value is now a function of how much his or her unique knowledge and skill can be multiplied by the constant application of new microtechnology.

This shift in the value of work from time-based to results-based measurement is another death blow to the philosophy and structure of the bureaucratic organization.

Microchip Law 6:

The microchip disintegrates all human work except creativity and relationship.

There is much written and discussed these days about the possible obsolescence of human beings by technology. If computers and robots can eventually replace any kind of human work, then how can anyone ever achieve economic security? Without productive work, how can anyone have a sense of meaning and personal value? But there is a much better, third question that hardly anyone is asking: *Are there any areas of the work world where machines will never replace humans?* The answer is a resounding yes.

Microtechnology, no matter how fast and powerful, will never replace two uniquely human capabilities: *the ability to create an infinite number of new things,* **and** *the ability to relate to other human beings in an infinite number of new ways.*

Creativity and relationship are the two abilities that make us uniquely human, and during the 21ˢᵗ century these are the only two areas of meaningful work that are safe from the encroachment of microchip-based tools, systems, and networks.

The application of microtechnology enhances the ability to create and to relate to those who are motivated, skilled, and

focused within these two fundamental areas of activity. But, at the same time, microtechnology will continually disintegrate and eliminate forms of work that are not based on increased creativity and expanded relationships.

This obviously has enormous implications for how children will be educated, how all workers in the economy will be trained and re-trained, and how all organizations in society will be structured and managed in the years ahead.

These six laws of the microchip, and others that may emerge in the coming decades, are now defining our foreknowledge of the global economy in four specific areas:

- Which industries will expand, and which will decline;
- Which type of organizations will prosper, and which will fail;
- Which economic skills in the marketplace will be rewarded, and which will be discarded; and
- Which forms of education and training will be crucial, and which will be obsolete.

We must stop reacting defensively to the specific advances of microtechnology, and begin mastering the laws of the microchip.

The only way for human beings to live successfully in a microchip-based economy is by aligning every aspect of their working and personal lives to these six fundamental laws. It is no longer the details of microtechnology that are important because these will always be changing at an exponential rate. The secret to success for all individuals and groups now lies in mastering and applying the underlying laws of the microchip to all areas of work and organization.

Coming back then to the subject of the life insurance industry in the microchip economy of the 21st century, two questions are crucial:

- **How will life insurance companies reorganize their structures to take advantage of the Pilzer's formula, Wealth = Resources x Technology?**

- **How will life insurance agents reorganize their professional practices so that their work consists of nothing except creativity and relationship?**

The answer to both questions lies in applying the six laws of the microchip to every aspect of company and agent activity over the next 25 years.

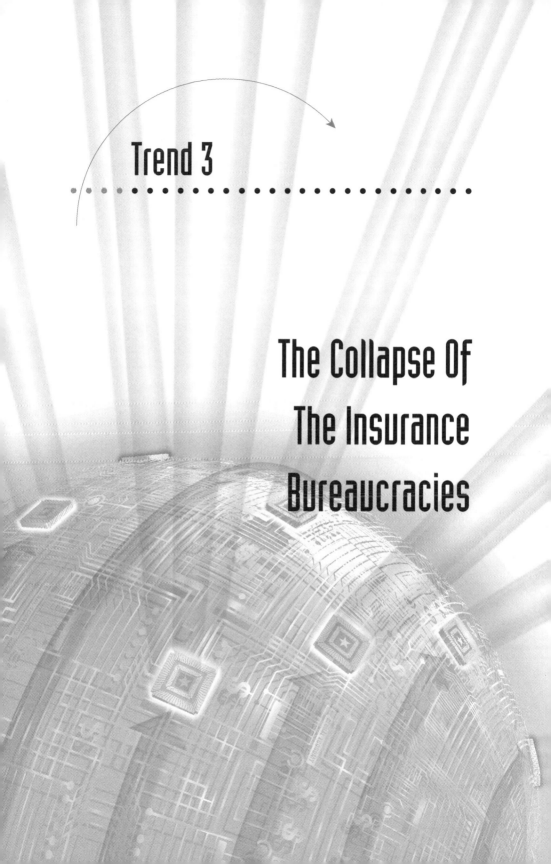

Trend 3

The Collapse Of The Insurance Bureaucracies

Trend 3

The Collapse Of The Insurance Bureaucracies

Here's an interesting comparison: three of the largest insurance companies in the U.S. and three of the largest mutual fund companies, at the end of 1993.

Two factors are considered: the amount of assets under management and the number of bureaucratic employees.

The life insurance companies are Prudential, Metropolitan, and New York Life. Prudential at the end of 1993 had $165.7 billion of assets under management and 76,776 employees. For Metropolitan, it was $126.2 billion and 31,639 and the figures for New York Life were $53.6 billion and 7,475 employees.

The three mutual fund companies are Merrill Lynch, Franklin Templeton, and Putnam. Merrill Lynch had $138 billion in assets and 1,057 employees. For Franklin Templeton, it was $113 billion and 3,603. And Putnam had $64 billion in assets, with 1,900 employees.

The average assets under management per employee for the three life insurance companies was $4.46 million, while for the three mutual fund companies it was $65.2 million! A comparison between one hundred other life insurance companies and one hundred other mutual fund companies would reveal a similar disparity.

The bottom line is simple: Life insurance companies are now just asset management companies and are in direct competition with mutual fund companies as well as all other asset management companies — banks, trusts, investment houses, and pension funds.

Increasingly, these organizations are all in the same business. All have exactly the same goals of 1.5 to 2% return on assets. And, increasingly they all have to play by the same set of organizational rules in a global economy based on microtechnology.

For life insurance companies around the world this means goodbye to bloated head offices and overly expensive career agency systems. But many companies are still trying to operate as things used to be.

During the period from 1945 to 1970, life was golden for most economic sectors in North America, and especially so for the life insurance industry. The Bretton Woods agreements following World War Two established a stable system of international finance, in which the U.S. enjoyed undisputed leadership and unprecedented prosperity. Corporations in all industries could grow almost without concern for costs because the market for products and services seemed unlimited. Huge bureaucracies, with multi-layers of middle managers, sprouted everywhere because the secret to increased profits during those 25 years was mass production and mass distribution.

It was almost impossible for life insurance companies to fail and even very difficult for them to have a bad year during that quarter century. There were only two life products to sell, whole life or term, and every company had more or less the same policies. That being the case, competitive advantage between companies lay mainly in making the head office bureaucracy and the career agency field force as big as possible.

But the world has changed drastically since the early 1970s, specifically because of the decision by President Nixon to disconnect the U.S. dollar from the gold standard in August 1971.

Trend 3

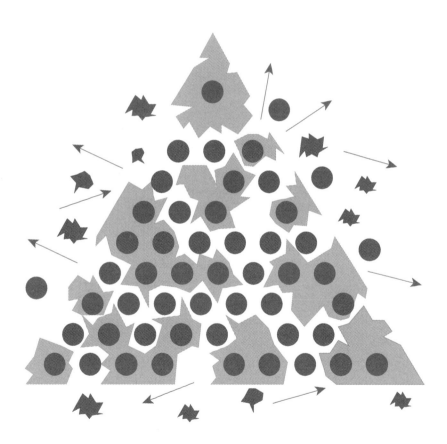

With the stroke of a pen, national economies in the non-communist world instantly became part of a single global economy where the manipulation of interest rates and currency rates from one country to the next caused massive and unpredictable flows of investment capital back and forth across national borders. It was at this historical juncture that the computer emerged as an extraordinarily powerful productivity and communications tool for investment houses, currency traders, and asset managers.

Within the financial services industry, competitive advantage began to be based on the six laws of the microchip. The mutual fund companies, because most of them were founded only recently, were in the best position to utilize microtechnology. Next came the investment houses. Then the banks. However, because the biggest of the bureaucracies had grown steadily in size within a protected environment throughout the 20th century, the life insurance companies were caught unprepared for this new economic reality.

The world became a 24-hour financial market, with trillions of dollars flowing through centers like London and New York on a daily basis. Very quickly, the central focus in the financial services industry became asset management. And throughout the 1980s, the regulatory walls that separated the various financial industries, and protected them from outside competition, began to disintegrate.

Which brings us to the 1990s, when all asset management companies in the world have come into direct competition with each other, which means there is now a continual race to be the leanest, most productive, most flexible, and most innovative organization.

In the life insurance industry, this is leading to a collapse of head office bureaucracies and, consequently, of career agency systems as they have existed until now. Because the life insurance industry is now just a subsystem of a much larger global financial industry, insurance companies will rapidly be forced to take on the form and structure of the most efficient and flexible financial organization in the global economy, *the mutual fund company*, which consists of a small head office staffed by well-paid specialists and supported by powerful software networks that link together thousands of entrepreneurial sales agents.

It is highly likely that an insurance company with $200 billion in assets under management in the year 2005 will have no more than 100 salaried personnel in its entire system. The biggest companies throughout the 21st century will be big only in terms of assets under management, not in bureaucratic structure.

In the 21st century insurance industry, there will be no such thing as a "safe" head office job, except one that is based on achieving entrepreneurial results. Hundreds of thousands of men and women who have bureaucratic jobs in the industry today — right up to the positions of president and chairman — will be "downsized" over the coming decade.

This will also include thousands of agency managers and general agents, whose roles will disappear as head offices become smaller and agents more entrepreneurial. Hundreds of companies will disappear in mergers, consolidations, and takeovers. Virtually all surviving companies will eliminate their career systems altogether and concentrate their distribution efforts on brokerage or mass media networks.

The bottom 40% of the insurance market will become an arena of fierce competition as other financial institutions, especially the banks, get into the game. As a result, up to 60% of the existing agents will be unable to earn a living on a commission basis. Those in this group who remain in the industry will do so as salaried insurance representatives for the competing financial institutions.

On the other hand, there are a growing number of entrepreneurial agents who have seen the handwriting on the wall over the past 10 years. They are taking steps to eliminate all dependence on bureaucratic relationships and structures.

In the process, they are discovering that there are also a growing number of forward-thinking insurance company executives who are prepared to enter into an entirely new partnership, one in which the

streamlined company sees a network of highly successful entrepreneurial agents as its key to the future.

**For the life insurance agent of today who plans not only to
survive but to thrive in this new environment, a number of
strategic attitudes are required:**

• *Recognize that the insurance companies — which are now
strictly asset management companies — will do everything possible to cut their costs of doing business with you.*
If you can help them do this, you will be a big hero, and a much bigger
entrepreneurial opportunity may emerge. Whatever the case, just remember
that the era of the "benevolent company that felt like a family" is long gone.

• *Be prepared for constant cutbacks in services and commissions.*
As the number of companies is reduced, a dozen or so mega-sized
companies will begin acting in concert to dictate compensation policies
for the whole industry. Large upfront commissions and bonuses will
soon be a thing of the past. Levelized commissions, asset management, and fee-based selling will be the way of the future — and much
sooner than most agents think.

• *Develop a worst case scenario in relation to each insurance
company — recognizing that it may not be able to live up to its
guarantees to you and your clients.*
Realize in all your dealings with head office personnel that your individual survival as an insurance agent is not one of their major priorities.

• *Don't take any of this personally.*
The future is on your side.
Simply accept that, as the global economy becomes more inte-
grated, insurance companies will become more susceptible to turmoil.
It's beyond anyone's control to prevent this. The forces of change are
too many and too powerful.

Trend 4

The Personal Electronic Insurance Company

Trend 4

Over the next two decades, productivity within the entire life insurance industry will be increasingly characterized by two technological factors:

- ***Software systems talking to software systems***:
  Agent software systems, anywhere in the world, talking to asset management software systems, everywhere in the world.

- ***The Personal Electronic Communicator (PEC)***:
  A hand-held computer with global communications capabilities. With this device, connected by wireless technology into a worldwide network of superb software systems, every entrepreneurial life insurance agent in the world will be able to have his or her own "personal electronic insurance company."

The PEC will be the result of the ongoing integration of many different microchip-based capabilities that already exist today. Inside this device will be immense computing power, in excess of 20 billion instructions per second (by 2005), combined with extraordinary actuarial, financial, management, and communications software programs that can design, process, implement, administer, and illustrate any insurance product or program.

As a result of this PEC capability, which will become more powerful on a yearly basis, the complex and lengthy underwriting process of today will be accomplished in minutes and hours, rather than weeks and months.

Using the global power of the PEC, the entrepreneurial agent will be able to bypass electronically nearly all of the bureaucratic structures, procedures, and functionaries that presently constitute "head office."

Probably as much as 95% of everything that makes up any bureaucratic organization today is ultimately programmable into a software capability that does not require the involvement of human managers and workers. Therefore, virtually all of the decision making required for normal processing of insurance policies — and claims — will be automated. This automation is coming quite quickly and will be widespread before the year 2000.

Obviously, from an agent's standpoint, the acceleration of the underwriting process will be a crucial breakthrough provided by the PEC technology, but there will be at least five other important benefits:

• *Electronic Global Access:*

By interfacing with the ever-expanding Internet (the global integration of millions of computer networks and databases), the entrepreneurial insurance agent will be able to tap into all insurance products, research, expertise, and markets in the world, *based on his or her own unique marketing strategies.*

• *Electronic Client Contact:*

In addition, he or she will be able to maintain real-time communications — software to software — with an entire client base. This will

Trend 4

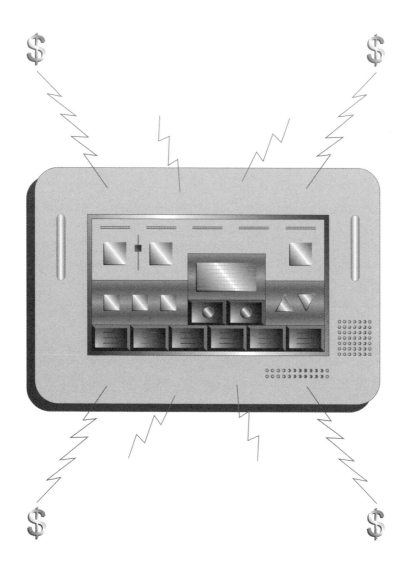

be accomplished with little or no expenditure of the agent's time as support staff are trained to administer routine client communications.

• *Electronic Expert Systems:*

Specialized capabilities, now the preserve of practitioners like lawyers, accountants, and doctors, will be available to entrepreneurial agents in the form of interactive software systems.

• *Electronic Producer Groups:*

The organization of large numbers of entrepreneurial agents into powerful, electronically-connected buying groups will enable individuals to negotiate with companies from a position of strength on matters of compensation, products, and services. This is a trend that is already underway and will be facilitated enormously by the PEC capability.

• *Electronic Teamwork:*

All communications, coordination, delegation, training, planning, and learning within an agent's own support team will be integrated and managed by having all personnel equipped with PECs.

These electronic capabilities already exist as possibilities for all life insurance agents, but in reality, only a small group of entrepreneurial agents will utilize them before the end of the 20ᵗʰ century.

Although much of the PEC technology already exists in separate devices, or is just around the corner in an integrated form, only a few agents today are actually in a position to take advantage of this extraordinary capability.

Technology, to be useful, requires not just the acquisition of equipment and technical competence, but a whole shift in thinking about how the world works. The following attitudes are especially important:

• **One, recognize that you will live increasingly in a universe of global electronic communication.**

Realize that the whole world is now connected through a "network of networks." This new electronic universe will transcend, disrupt, and integrate all other non-electronic structures and systems in global society.

The entire global economy is going electronic faster than anyone can comprehend, with millions of entrepreneurs and organizations plugging into the Internet on a monthly basis. A whole new economic universe is coming into existence with its own realities and rewards. The ability to navigate within this universe and to create value within *a network of networks* is now the key to personal and professional success, especially for anyone involved in the marketing of life insurance products and services.

It is necessary, therefore, to be prepared for a life insurance industry where everything except the sale happens electronically, and where the failure of an agent to operate electronically means exclusion from the industry.

• **Two, be aware of how microchip technology can enhance your productivity on a continual basis.**

Recognize that understanding of certain microchip capabilities is now as important as insurance knowledge. Operating an insurance practice without PEC technology by the year 2005 will be as unthinkable as operating without a telephone would have been in 1990.

This does not mean that a life insurance agent becomes a technological expert, but rather that he or she knows how to utilize the abilities of individuals who are skilled in both hardware and software — especially those who are skilled in software related to the insurance industry.

It is now necessary for entrepreneurial agents to develop a support team of experts who continually assist them in creating a microchip future for the personal electronic insurance company. The basis for planning and implementing this future will be the six laws of the microchip listed in Trend 2.

• **Three, surround yourself increasingly with skilled practitioners of electronic communication.**

There is now a whole generation of younger individuals, under age 25, for whom electronic communication is as natural as handwriting is for older people. Most of these men and women are self-taught. Many of them, recognizing that the school system was incapable of preparing them for opportunity in an electronic economy, began playing with computers when they were adolescents, and now find they have highly marketable skills.

As an entrepreneurial agent in the 21ˢᵗ century, it is necessary for you to continually seek out and hire these individuals as members of your personal electronic insurance company.

Then, through a constant training program for these individuals, continue to add new microchip-based capabilities. See all of your organizational growth and progress over the remainder of your career being supported by increased electronic communications.

• **Four, recognize that over the next 25 years everything that you do except what relates to creativity and relationship can be handled by your evolving electronic support team.**

Even though some people still deny it, it is now a reality of the bureaucratic world that there is no such thing as *job* security. Anyone doing predictable bureaucratic work, no matter what their rank or job description, will ultimately be replaced as a result of the constant evolution of microchip-based technologies.

In fact, as we move into the 21ˢᵗ century, there are only two human activities that cannot be replaced by technology: creativity and relationship.

No matter how powerful and fast microchips become, and no matter how "smart" the devices seem to be, they will never replace the human ability to create new economic value and the ability to relate to other human beings in a creative fashion.

Therefore, as an entrepreneurial agent in this new electronic universe, focus all your time and attention on creative economic relationships that are totally supported by superb electronic capabilities.

Trend 5

The Unlimited Entrepreneurial Market

Trend 5

• •

As microtechnology and "the laws of the microchip" continue to transform the life insurance industry, there will be a widening gulf among all life insurance agents between two classes — *the "haves" and the "have-nots."*

By 2005, the **haves** will be those experienced agents, numbering around 10,000 and making in excess of $500,000 personal income per year, who operate as complete entrepreneurial companies, making use of microtechnology to multiply their resources and results. There will be, in addition, another 10,000 younger agents who have the capability of reaching this level of success.

The **have-nots** will be those agents, seldom making more than $75,000, who will try to hang on to the old approaches, methods, procedures, and structures of the collapsing bureaucratic "career" system. These individuals will number in the hundreds of thousands, and most of them will be on a salaried contract.

Besides the use of microtechnology itself, the biggest determining factor separating the haves from the have-nots among insurance agents over the next 25 years will be the differing nature of their client bases.

GLOBAL STATUS SYSTEM™ THROUGHOUT THE 21ˢᵗ CENTURY	
1	**Global Entrepreneurs**
2	**National Entrepreneurs**
3	**Local Entrepreneurs**
4	**Entrepreneurial Support**
5	**Entrepreneurial Dependents**
6	**Bureaucratic Executives**
7	**Bureaucratic Managers**
8	**Bureaucratic Workers**
9	**Bureaucratic Dependents**
10	**Bureaucratic Rejects**

The have agents will have entrepreneurs as clients, while the have-not agents will continue to seek clients among those individuals who are caught up in the rapidly diminishing opportunities of the bureaucratic world.

Here it is necessary to examine a fundamental reality about the economic, political, and social world of the 21st century: that there is now a global status system forming on the basis of entrepreneurial attitude, capability, and opportunity.

The diagram on the previous page lists 10 different levels of participation in this new status system. Those at the top of the system have the greatest access to economic capabilities, resources, and opportunities. Those at the bottom have the least.

This is not just an economic status system, but one that also defines the political, social, and cultural status of individuals and groups for at least the next 100 years. Throughout the 21st century, virtually all public debate of issues in all countries will revolve around the inequalities of participation in this ten-level hierarchy of power, influence, and advantage.

From top to bottom, here is an explanation of each of these categories:

- *Level 1: Global Entrepreneurs*
These are economically autonomous individuals who operate successfully across national borders. In essence, they have escaped from the world of bureaucratic politics, for they are able to plan their future growth to take advantage of the most promising markets in any part of the world, at short notice.

Governments are now subject to the ambitions and activities of these individuals as a collective group, rather than the other way around. Global entrepreneurs are the lead force in the spread of microtechnology around the world.

On an opportunity scale of 10, these individuals score a 10.

• **Level 2: National Entrepreneurs**

These are economically autonomous individuals who operate within a large market but still within the borders of one country. Depending on the population base, they enjoy increased advantages and opportunities because of the application of microtechnology to all sectors of the national economy.

On an opportunity scale of 10, these individuals score 7.5.

• **Level 3: Local Entrepreneurs**

Economically autonomous individuals who operate within a local market area or territory. Depending on the product or service being sold, they are vulnerable to downturns in the local economy and are the most subject of all entrepreneurs to the policies of bureaucratic organizations, especially governments.

For the past ten years, these entrepreneurs have created the greatest number of new jobs and business tax revenues in most national economies.

On an opportunity scale of 10, these individuals score 5.

• **Level 4: Entrepreneurial Support**

Individuals who work in an entrepreneurial company to support the money-making activities of the key entrepreneurs. They are usually salary-based but can greatly increase their compensation through bonuses and profit-sharing. Their efforts, rewards, and opportunities are directly tied to the results achieved by the whole organization.

On an opportunity scale of 10, these individuals score 4.

• **Level 5: Entrepreneurial Dependents**

Individuals, usually spouses and children without independent income, who depend on an entrepreneurial individual for their economic security.

On an opportunity scale of 10, these individuals score 3.

• **Level 6: Bureaucratic Executives**

Individuals who strategically plan and manage bureaucratic organizations. Although these individuals may have considerable power, status, and compensation within the organization, forces in the global marketplace can remove them from their positions in an unpredictable manner, usually at very short notice.

Some of these individuals have excellent entrepreneurial capabilities, but never find out until they are fired or quit. Those who do not have entrepreneurial capabilities can drop all the way down to Level 10.

On an opportunity scale of 10, these individuals score 2.5.

• *Level 7: Bureaucratic Managers*

Individuals in the "middle" of a bureaucratic organization who are responsible for hiring, training, managing, and firing bureaucratic workers. In some industries, life insurance being one example, these bureaucratic managers can also interact directly with entrepreneurs. This is an increasingly thankless and precarious job in the age of the microchip.

Over the past 10 years, a large number of these individuals have been forced out of bureaucracy and into the entrepreneurial marketplace, and this trend will continue at an accelerated rate, especially in the service industries and government.

On an opportunity scale of 10, these individuals score 1.5.

• *Level 8: Bureaucratic Workers*

Individuals who, for the time being, have salaried employment (a job description) within a bureaucratic organization.

There is continual uncertainty and insecurity at this level because of the global trend to replace human labor with microchip-based devices and systems.

On an opportunity scale of 10, these individuals score 1.

• *Level 9: Bureaucratic Dependents*

Individuals, usually spouses and children without income, who are dependent upon someone with a bureaucratic job for their economic welfare.

On an opportunity scale of 10, these individuals score 0.5.

• *Level 10: Bureaucratic Rejects*
These are individuals with no entrepreneurial capabilities who have been rejected for employment within bureaucratic structures. Essentially, they are at the mercy of government or charitable organizations for their economic survival.
On an opportunity scale of 10, these individuals score 0.1.

The wealthiest, most influential individuals on the planet throughout the 21ˢᵗ century will be highly successful entrepreneurs (Levels 1 to 3) who share a creative philosophy toward their life and work and who are interconnected electronically across political borders.

Many of the products and services that will dominate the global economy 10 years from now have not yet been invented. Many of the most important companies of the early 21ˢᵗ century have not yet been formed. And many of the industries that will show the greatest promise a decade from now are not yet in existence.

Increasingly, an individual's status in society, and his or her economic possibilities, will be determined by the degree of participation in entrepreneurial activity.

By the same token, life insurance agents will be successful over the next 25 years to the degree that their clients are concentrated in Levels 1 to 5.

By 2005, half the population of the United States will derive their income from entrepreneurial activities. As far as Levels 6 to 10 go, there will be a constant diminishing of economic resources and opportunity, and these sectors of the population will decrease continually.
A life insurance agent cannot effectively tap into this unlimited entrepreneurial market until he or she is a complete entrepreneur in attitude, organization, and results. It takes one to know one.

The life insurance agents who become the counselors, coaches, and problem solvers for the best entrepreneurs in the world during the 21st century will be those who have separated themselves from all bureaucratic dependencies.

- Develop a complete entrepreneurial growth model for each client. Realize that the concept of an entrepreneurial career will become more ordinary than the concept of a bureaucratic career.

- Take advantage of the unlimited growth potential of entrepreneurs. As microtechnology expands through hundreds of new devices, systems, and integrated networks, the opportunities for entrepreneurial growth become unlimited.

- Develop a mastery of all key issues facing entrepreneurs.

- Become each entrepreneurial client's most important lifetime advisor.

- Realize that opportunities for entrepreneurial clients will grow exponentially over the next 25 years.

- Transform your client base so that it consists entirely of successful, ambitious entrepreneurs who are taking advantage of microtechnology. The key to the formation of a successful insurance practice is to have only individuals who have multiple insurance needs for the future.

- Become an economic specialist to a network of successful entrepreneurs.

- Recognize that entrepreneurial futures now have greater predictability than bureaucratic futures.

- See yourself growing exponentially as a result of the exponential growth of your entrepreneurial clients.

The global status system described on the previous pages is something that many people would rather not think about. There is still a powerful tendency for most people to see the world in political terms, as things being a matter of the political right versus the political left, or conservative versus liberal.

Most public leaders, including those in the news media, have not yet grasped that the political framework that has governed public discourse and debate for hundreds of years is now meaningless for describing the divisions in society.

The only meaningful division is now the entrepreneurial versus the bureaucratic. All other explanations of the stratification of society are subordinate to this one, which is economic rather than political. The ability to succeed and prosper no longer has much to do with political belief or affiliation; it has mainly to do with entrepreneurial attitudes and capabilities.

Those who understand this new status system in the 1990s are ahead of the global game, because it could very well be another 50 years before the general population begins to think and plan within this new framework.

In the meantime, there are many worlds to be created and many fortunes to be made by those who detect important things early.

Trend 6

Breaking Through
The Ceiling
Of Complexity™

Trend 6

- -
Breaking Through The Ceiling Of Complexity™

Ten percent of agents in the world today have never had it so good. For these strategically-focused men and women — *The 21st Century Agents* — the next 25 year period is going to be the best of all possible economic worlds.

As they look ahead to the unlimited entrepreneurial opportunity of the 21st century, they can see a clear upward path to extraordinary professional success, personal growth, and enhanced quality of life. They know where they're going, why they're going, and how to get there.

For the remaining 90% of life insurance agents in the 1990s, however, it's a different story. As they look ahead to the rest of the decade, they see nothing but uncertainty, complications, and trouble.

They are finding their progress increasingly blocked by a *"ceiling of complexity."* They want to go higher but somehow they can't. An invisible barrier to performance prevents them from achieving higher quality sales and higher levels of commission income.

Here's what this ceiling of complexity looks like: an agent experiences several years of significant growth, makes the President's Club, makes MDRT, then hits a plateau. For top agents this happens first at $125,000 personal income, then at $250,000, at $500,000, again at $1 million, and finally at $2 million. Beyond the $2-million ceiling, it's usually clear sailing.

Let's look at the first ceiling of complexity, at $125,000:

Because virtually all agents have been trained within some kind of career agency system, the emphasis is on activity. Inexperienced agents are told to see as many people as possible, to do as many fact-finders as possible, and to write as many applications as possible.

If an individual has good work habits, good time management, and can withstand large doses of rejection, he or she can get up to the $125,000 level in a few years. Each year sees an increase of 25% over the year before. There is enormous excitement. The opportunities are getting bigger; the cases are getting bigger. Within the agency system, the agent is seen as a rising star and is given special attention and praise at company meetings. He or she is sent on the road to speak at agency meetings and company conventions.

But then the progress suddenly stops. The first year, the income is $125,000. The next year it's $130,000, then it drops to $115,000, and for three or four years it never gets any higher than $135,000.

The agent has hit the first ceiling of complexity. And there is nothing in his or her training within the life insurance industry that indicates what to do next. There are two main causes of this ceiling, one having to do with the structure of the life insurance industry, the other having to do with the way that life insurance agents create their own organization in the marketplace.

• First cause of the ceiling of complexity: the economics, management, and mentality of the life insurance industry.

From a head office perspective, any agent who makes $125,000 per year is an extraordinary success. On a worldwide basis, fewer than 5% of active agents ever hit this level of personal income during the course of their careers. As a matter of fact, once any agent gets above $100,000, he or she is usually perceived as something of a threat by

Trend 6

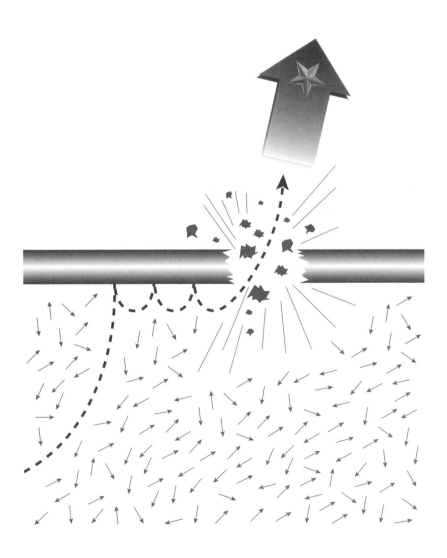

the insurance company. If the truth were told, most life insurance companies would like to have thousands of agents selling an average of
150 lives per year, none of them personally making more than
$60,000.

There are several reasons for this:

1. Costs and risks.

As agents become more successful, the nature of their cases
becomes more sophisticated and complex, and therefore more costly
and risky to the company from an underwriting and administrative
standpoint. It takes longer for the company to show a profit. Therefore,
there is a natural tendency for head offices to favor thousands of small
cases, which can be processed at lower costs, rather than fewer large
cases. The entire mentality of the bureaucratic system is geared to
mass marketing and processing rather than customized sales.

2. Irrelevance.

Many of the individuals who become agency managers and general agents were not extraordinary salespeople themselves, and
therefore do not have much personal experience of achieving high
income as agents. They get most of their compensation as managers
from recruiting and training new agents, 90% of whom are not in
the industry after five years. And they tend to operate on regimented
methods of training and management that are understandable and
reassuring to bureaucratic executives at head office, but are irrelevant to the growth requirements of agents making more than
$100,000.

3. Resentment.

Very few individuals at head office make more than $100,000,
and those who do have put up with long years of bureaucratic tedium,
pressure, and frustration to get there. The fact that some agents, after
only two or three years in the business, can get to this level and far
beyond it can be a source of resentment throughout the bureaucratic

ranks. The fact that certain agents can make double or triple the income of the CEO of the insurance company can be a source of *enormous* resentment.

Head office resentment of the successful agent is seldom expressed openly but rather through a subtle web of non-cooperation and bureaucratic entanglement: delays in underwriting service and decision making, complicated new policies and procedures, product restrictions and discontinuations, decreases in compensation, withdrawal of administrative support, and invitations to serve without pay on head office committees, task forces, and panels that go on endlessly and accomplish nothing of value for the agent.

In short, the life insurance industry as a whole significantly reduces its material and psychological support to agents once they pass the $100,000 level of personal income.

And this is why, over the past decade, tens of thousands of successful agents have left the career system. Unless there is an unusually enlightened head office, and an unusually competent agency manager or General Agent, it makes more sense — theoretically — for $100,000+ agents to operate as independent brokers.

• Second cause of the ceiling of complexity: the way that life insurance agents organize themselves in the marketplace.

Although technically speaking all commissioned agents are entrepreneurs, most of them don't think and act like entrepreneurs. They try to play an entrepreneur's game using a set of rules and methods that were designed for the administrative benefit of bureaucratic personnel at head office.

In running their businesses, unfortunately most agents still see themselves as *managers of complexity:* a mental image that embroils them in many of the same bureaucratic methods, processes, and structures that they were trying to escape. They try to be the little CEO of a little bureaucratic company.

They frequently become "control freaks" within their own operation, unable to delegate properly and insisting on being involved in everything, making all decisions, and checking everything for quality control. As their businesses grow, they become increasingly bogged down in the complexities of administration, an area of skill where they are generally incompetent.

These bureaucratic chores increasingly prevent them from doing the one thing they are uniquely good at: *creating and selling unique financial solutions to individuals with unique problems and opportunities.*

As the years go by, experienced agents find themselves bogged down more and more in administration and spending less and less of their time actually selling or marketing.

These individuals have enormous opportunities beckoning, but they can't take advantage of them because of the ceiling of complexity they have created for themselves through their own bureaucratic attitudes and involvements.

The most successful entrepreneurial agents break through the ceiling of complexity by focusing on a series of strategies that free them from everything except creativity and relationship.

The second part of this book consists of 20 strategies that enable entrepreneurial agents to break through the ceiling of complexity. On the one hand, these strategies keep the agent free from the bureaucratic entanglements and obstacles caused by head office structures, processes, and turmoil. On the other hand, these 20 strategies enable an agent to escape from the complexities caused by his or her own organizational history and activities.

The purpose of these strategies is to create a permanent operating vehicle for the agent where he or she can be focused entirely on creativity and relationship and have all other aspects of the business handled by superb support people and systems.

Taken together, these 20 strategies — once they become a matter of daily decision making, action, and habit — are the structure of The 21ˢᵗ Century Agent.

Strategy 1

Focus On Your Own Quality Of Life, And Let Your Income Match It

Strategy 1

Focus On Your Own Quality Of Life, And Let Your Income Match It

Many agents in the past have made financial objectives their sole concern and have paid a heavy price for their success — poor health, failed marriages, neglected friendships, and no personal development in any area except business.

Financial success, no matter how great, can never compensate for poor quality of life. In the scheme of things, a properly functioning business is supposed to be the servant of a full and satisfactory life that includes good health, close and loving relationships, recreation, culture, and a powerful contribution to the community.

The 21st Century Agent will develop a personal life that is multidimensional and characterized by an ever-increased quality of experience, while increasing his or her income continually to support that quality.

This first strategy is the foundation for all the others. An insurance career, no matter how successful, is just one dimension of a whole lifetime. And if that lifetime is to be a happy and satisfying one, it must have many more dimensions besides a successful insurance career.

At the same time, the life insurance agent who is multidimensional in his or her approach to life never suffers any loss of opportunity or income because of his or her interests and involvements in other things besides business.

That's because quality of life attracts quality of life. Individuals who are multidimensional attract other individuals who are multidimensional.

The agent who establishes a lifetime perspective that includes many different dimensions of experience will communicate a quality of life that makes him or her highly attractive to the very best kind of clients, support staff, and centers of influence.

Life insurance agents, among all business practitioners, should be the most multidimensional in their interests. That's because, of all professions in the world, agents are able to ask questions about every aspect of a prospect's or client's life. No one gets to ask the range of human interest questions that an agent asks — not lawyers, not accountants, not doctors, not members of the clergy. Agents get to ask about everything. In fact, they *must* ask about everything in order to create the appropriate insurance protection.

This is one of the main reasons why clients are loyal to insurance agents, but not to insurance companies. The agent, if he or she is a multidimensional person, is the one who assists the client in thinking clearly about the deepest issues of the future, including the consequences of death and disability.

It is the agent who assists the client in making crucial decisions about taxation, investments, retirement, inheritance, business partnerships and succession, charitable giving, and benefits for employees. All of these take into account the client's purpose in business and in life, his or her values, interests, and, ultimately, his or her significance as a human being.

Strategy 1

The more multidimensional you are in your own life, the more you will be able to connect with all the dimensions of each of your clients' lives. And your income will naturally and significantly increase to match this lifetime process of experimentation, discovery, learning, and growth.

In order to keep this multidimensional strategy in mind, here are several things to remember:

• **Recognize that you will judge yourself by your whole life, not just your career.**

When you get to the end of your life, you won't be judging yourself on premium sales and commission dollars, renewals and persistency, or President's Club or Top Of The Table. Rather, you will be looking at how you handled your relationships, how you developed your abilities, how you followed up on your interests in life, and how much you gave back to your many communities.

• **Compile a list of everything extraordinary that you want to do in your life, and strive to achieve each item.**

Schedule these extraordinary achievements over the course of an entire lifetime. Every year complete four or five things that you've dreamed about doing. In the course of your lifetime, you will develop a wealth of experience in many different areas. You will meet a wide diversity of human beings, and you will have mastered a wide range of different abilities.

• **Create a strategy of giving back to everyone and everything in your life.**

Establish yourself as a creative benefactor in every area of your life. Always give back for everything that you receive. Other people immediately recognize this quality and find it not only attractive but inspiring. To bring inspiration into the lives of others, and to do so in a unique and interesting manner based on many different kinds of life experience, is perhaps the greatest gift that anyone can provide over the course of a lifetime.

Strategy 2

Focus On Being
An Entrepreneur, With
A Specialty
In Life Insurance

Strategy 2

Focus On Being An Entrepreneur, With A Specialty In Life Insurance

No one really knows what the insurance industry will look like 10 years from now, but one thing is certain — the most successful life insurance agents will be those who approach the marketplace first and foremost as entrepreneurs. That is, they will see themselves as problem solvers for their clients rather than as peddlers of products for the insurance companies.

An entrepreneur is not tied to any particular method of selling. He or she does not try to impose any particular kind of product or service on the consumer. Rather, as an entrepreneur, he or she creates the product or service based largely on the needs, desires, goals, and aspirations of the insurance customer.

The 21st Century Agent will be a constantly improving entrepreneur who happens to have a specialty in life insurance.

This distinction is true of all other professions as well. For example, there are lawyers, and then there are entrepreneurs who have a specialty in law. There are accountants, and there are entrepreneurs who have a specialty in accounting. On the doorstep of the 21st century, specialized training is no longer the crucial factor in determining professional growth and success. *Being an entrepreneur is.*

Whether any kind of specialized expertise has any value in today's economy depends increasingly upon whether the person who provides the expertise thinks and acts like an entrepreneur.

Here are several things to focus your thinking about being an entrepreneurial life insurance agent over the next 25 years:

• **Recognize that an entrepreneur is someone who has made two fundamental choices in life.**

One, he or she chooses to depend entirely upon personal abilities as the basis for economic security for the future.

No ability, no security. This is a radical contrast to the bureaucratic mentality which looks for lifetime security by being part of "the system." Personal success everywhere is increasingly based on self-responsibility, not organizational status. Personal advancement is increasingly based on a process of self-designed learning and improvement of skills. Money, power, and influence are increasingly a direct result of self-created knowledge and capabilities.

Two, the person who is an entrepreneur chooses not to expect any economic opportunity in life until he or she has first created value for someone else.

No value, no opportunity. Again, this is a radical departure from the bureaucratic attitude that has permeated modern societies for the past 60 years in which people felt entitled to opportunity throughout their lives regardless of whether they created anything or not, regardless of whether they contributed anything or not. The entrepreneurial individual recognizes that in today's world there is unlimited opportunity to create value for others. He or she does not expect anyone else to create opportunity and therefore puts all personal focus on creating value for others.

• **Recognize that, in a world of rapid change, the fundamental structure of being an entrepreneur always remains the same.**

An entrepreneur living in 1500 and an entrepreneur in 2500 would completely understand each other. Entrepreneurs in any situation

Strategy 2

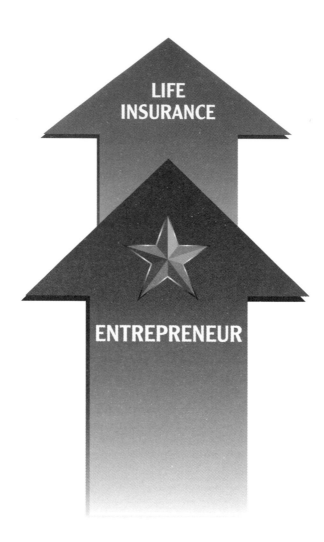

always understand entrepreneurs in every other situation regardless of differences in race, gender, age, religion, education, culture, political systems, or geographic location.

People who are employed in bureaucracies are constantly being forced to change their structures and methods, usually in response to the latest management philosophy or fad. In today's world, bureaucratic managers and workers frequently don't know from one year to the next what is going to happen to their job descriptions, their reporting structures, their functional skills, or the organization itself.

Entrepreneurial abilities, methods, and structures, on the other hand, are never threatened or outmoded by any kind of change. Just the opposite is true. The entrepreneurial structure, which is timeless and universal in nature, feeds on change rather than being disrupted by it. The more things change, the stronger and more integrated the entrepreneurial structure becomes.

• Accept that the life insurance industry will be a constantly changing structure over the next 25 years — and take advantage of it.

The life insurance industry as it exists in 1995, from an organizational standpoint, will be unrecognizable in 2020.

At the very beginning of these next 25 years, adopt a completely entrepreneurial structure that keeps you safe from the organizational crises and turmoil of the the insurance bureaucracies. Then, over the next 25 years, continually put yourself in a strategic position to take advantage of insurance company troubles. The greater the organizational troubles at head office, the greater the creative opportunities for the entrepreneurial agent.

As an entrepreneurial agent, be a catalyst for creating an entirely new industry based on entrepreneurial principles. See yourself as part of the creative force that is transforming the global insurance industry.

Strategy 3

Focus On Autonomy, And Treat Insurance Companies Strictly As Suppliers

Strategy 3

Focus On Autonomy And Treat Insurance Companies Strictly As Suppliers

The word "autonomy" means to live by your own laws. It comes from two ancient Greek words: *autos* = self, *nomos* = law. Therefore, *autos* + *nomos* = self-law. Individuals who establish and live by their own self-laws are autonomous. They are able to live and act independently in a world where most other people experience lives of dependency, especially bureaucratic dependency.

For the life insurance agent in the 21st century this will mean establishing self-laws which enable him or her to operate independently from the bureaucratic control of life insurance companies.

What does this independence entail? Two things.

First of all, emotional and psychological independence, wherein the agent stops expecting the companies to be "caring" or "supportive" or concerned about his or her welfare and success. Secondly, financial and management independence, wherein the agent takes total responsibility for operating overhead and infrastructure — and stops looking for subsidies, hand-outs, or special deals from the insurance companies.

The 21st Century Agent will see his or her insurance practice as an autonomous, self-sustaining, stand-alone enterprise that deals with insurance companies strictly as suppliers.

There are still a surprising number of successful agents who are emotionally, psychologically, financially, and organizationally dependent upon a particular company. This may have made sense at an earlier period of their careers, but in the 1990s this dependency is the biggest barrier to their future success and security. This is true not only within the insurance industry but throughout all other industries in the global economy.

As global society crosses over from the age of politics to the age of economics, the smartest path for all human beings is towards autonomy, especially economic autonomy. Life insurance agents, of all people, should be in the forefront of this trend.

Here are three things to think about:

• Recognize that your main security lies in an independent enterprise.

In a world where political structures can no longer protect and reassure individuals as they have in the past, establishing, maintaining, and expanding economic autonomy are now the most important abilities for all men, women, and children on the planet. This means being an entrepreneur. This means eliminating all dependency on bureaucracies. Over the next hundred years, having an entrepreneurial business is the single most important organizational structure for developing all the abilities necessary for economic autonomy.

In a global economy where power is based increasingly on personal economic autonomy, a new educational system based on entrepreneurial principles will gradually emerge and dominate public values and determine public structures, especially government. In the same way that children throughout the 20ᵗʰ century learned to work and succeed in large bureaucracies, children in the 21ˢᵗ century will learn to be autonomous economically.

Status in the global economy of the 21ˢᵗ century is a function of participation in entrepreneurial activity and organizations.

• Establish criteria for judging the long-range quality of insurance companies.

Strategy 3

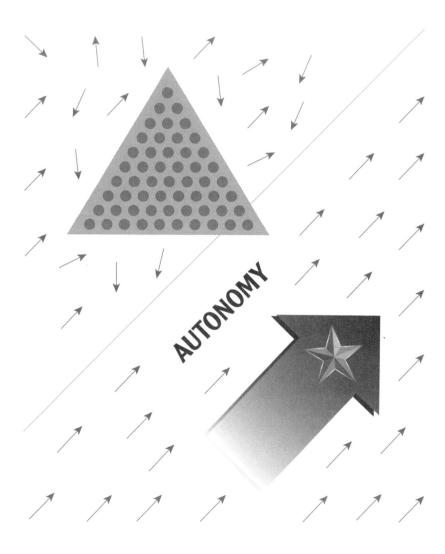

AUTONOMY

In their book *Built To Last*, authors James Collins and Jerry Porras identify the four successful habits of visionary companies: adherence to core values, audacious goals that are beyond present capabilities, a perspective that transcends the profit motive, and constant innovation of new products and services. Companies that have these habits are autonomous within the global economy. They are able to control their own development while thousands of other companies are failing or being taken over.

Over the next 25 years, life insurance agents must look for strategic alliances with companies that are still going to be in business in 2020, and the four qualities above are excellent criteria when comparing insurance companies.

In other words, autonomous agents must link up with autonomous companies. They must scrutinize the companies as if they were stocks in the securities market and then make investments based on the concept of a continual, high rate of return over 25 years.

• Join producer groups of hundreds and thousands of autonomous agents.

A natural consequence of the upheavals within the life insurance industry over the past decade has been the emergence of *producer groups*. These are federations of autonomous life insurance agents who have chosen to band together to provide themselves with the economies of scale of an insurance company without the bureaucratic limitations of the career agency systems. Some of the more prominent producer groups in the United States are The Partners Group, M Financial Group, and The Hemisphere Group. One hundred or more autonomous agents, joined in a producer group, can negotiate more powerfully with insurance companies than can a single agent. Take advantage of the collective power of agents in the marketplace. Microtechnology creates the possibility of extraordinarily powerful producer groups. Recognize that you are the buyer and the insurance companies are the seller. Demand that the companies treat you like an important customer. Stop looking for subsidies and special favors as an individual; instead cut a collective deal that reinforces your personal autonomy.

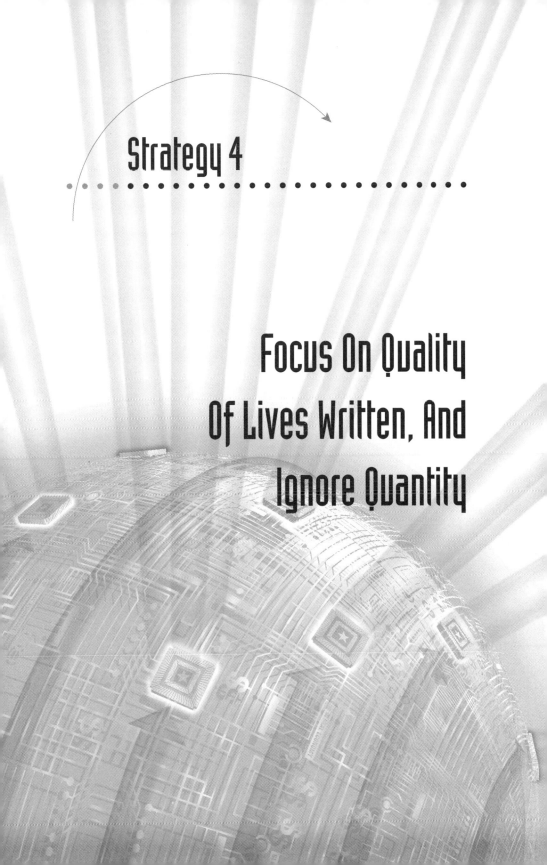

Strategy 4

Focus On Quality Of Lives Written, And Ignore Quantity

Strategy 4

For 150 years life insurance has been seen by life insurance compa-nies as a mass distribution product. This is still the case. Agents are praised and rewarded for the *quantity* of individual lives written each year, with little regard given to the nature of the clients, other than that they are insurable and that the policies stay on the books.

This system worked fine for the agent as long as commissions were high, and as long as the insurance companies were willing to underwrite the cost of servicing the complex requirements of the large number of cases in the agent's client base. That is no longer the case. Agents are still being asked to focus on quantity, but the com-panies are cutting back drastically on service support as well as com-pensation.

The 21ˢᵗ Century Agent will ignore the quantity requirements of the insurance companies, focusing instead on providing superb solutions and service to a smaller number of high quality clients who are repeat buyers and who provide high quality referrals.

This doesn't mean that quantity of lives isn't important, just that it can't be the agent's primary focus. At the beginning of an agent's career, it's important to write a higher number of cases each year, for two reasons. One, the average premium sales for an inexperienced agent are lower, so more policies must be sold to achieve a decent income. Two, the agent needs to have several hundred successful sales just to get a feel for the business.

For the first five years of an agent's career, achieving over one hundred successful applications per year probably represents a necessary and useful process. But then there must be a significant shift in focus, away from quantity of lives and on to quality of lives.

There are three things to think about:

• **Recognize that your greatest asset is the future growth capability of your best 40 clients.**
This means that right now you have certain relationships that are far more important than others.

In fact, in any life agent's client base there are 40 existing relationships that, from the standpoint of future income and opportunities, are worth more than all the other relationships combined.

If the agent would focus increasingly on these 40 relationships as the basis of new business, and as a source of high quality referrals, he or she could literally give all the other relationships away to other agents and make a lot more money in the process.

In The Strategic Coach Program, we have had agents cut their client base from 600 down to 100 and have seen them increase their income by 50% in each of the next three years. We have many agents come into the Program averaging 160 – 200 lives per year who have never made more than $125,000 in their career. In the first year, by focusing on quality rather than quantity, their number of lives drops to 90, and their income jumps to $200,000.

The reason is simple: by pruning their existing client base, and then focusing much more time, attention, and creativity on their best remaining 40 clients, they are increasingly introduced to much higher quality opportunities.

Strategy 4

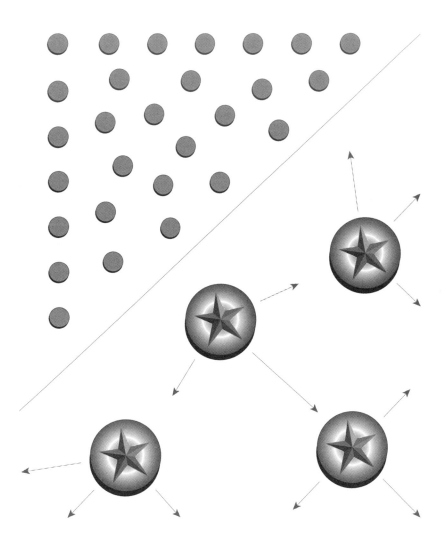

©1995, The Strategic Coach Inc.

• **Delegate or refer client relationships that do not align with your future growth.**

As an agent, it's not your biggest and best clients who eat up your time but the smallest — the ones who will probably never buy again and who have never given you good referrals. Therefore, in order to jump to the next level of performance and income, you must free yourself from the time, expense, and obligations involved in non-growth situations.

Recognize that most of your existing clients (all but the top 40) represent your past — a past stage of learning which must be left behind. Every non-growth relationship that you continue servicing increases your cost of doing business while blocking you from further growth.

There are two ways of handling this situation: one, train a licensed staff person or junior agent to handle these situations so that no more of your time is Involved; or two, recommend to these clients that they go to another agent, and give them a list of references.

• **Focus on developing an inventory of high quality "human futures" that will create unlimited growth.**

Right now, all the income that you will need for the remainder of your career will be available to you over time within the network of hundreds of individuals and organizations connected to your 40 best existing relationships. If you're willing to focus on the best forty that you have, you will continually be introduced to other equally high quality individuals and opportunities.

The question is: Where are your best "human futures"? Do an inventory, and separate the growth relationships from the non-growth. Delegate or eliminate the non-growth clients. Then identify the top 40 growth relationships, and focus 80% of your ongoing marketing time on these individuals, and on their referrals.

If you do this, your income will jump 25% to 50% in the first 12 months, and your life as an insurance agent will be significantly more simple, stimulating, and satisfying.

Strategy 5

Focus On The Entrepreneurial Markets, And Avoid The Bureaucrats

Strategy 5

- -

Focus On The Entrepreneurial Markets, And Avoid The Bureaucrats

It used to be that some of the best life insurance prospects were exec-utives, managers, and senior employees of large corporations and other large bureaucratic organizations. But microtechnology is now destroying the rationale for large bureaucracies, so that millions of bureaucratic executives and workers no longer have a predictable financial future.

At the same time, microtechnology has created enormous opportu-nities for millions of entrepreneurs, who now have extraordinary per-sonal and business futures that will require major insurance underwriting.

The 21ˢᵗ Century Agent will focus increasingly on the entrepreneurial market and avoid the declining prospects and unpredictability of bureaucratic clients and their organizations.

"There is a tide in the affairs of men
Which, taken at the flood, leads on to fortune;
Omitted, all the voyage of their life
Is bound in shallows and in miseries."

This passage from Shakespeare perfectly sums up the emerging global economy of the 21st century; the "tide" being the microchip revolution that favors entrepreneurial businesses of every nature; the "shallows and miseries" being the lack of security and opportunity experienced by millions of bureaucratic individuals who lack the entrepreneurial attitudes necessary to cope with global changes.

It also sums up the differences between the haves and the havenots among life insurance agents — those who focus on entrepreneurs as their clients, and those who are involved mainly with bureaucratic clients and prospects.

Over the next 25 years, there will be unlimited opportunity for those agents who strategically focus their marketing efforts on the rising tide of entrepreneurism.

Here are several guidelines for accomplishing this:

• **Sort your client base into two groups: entrepreneurs and bureaucrats.**

On the one hand, recognize that your bureaucratic clients face an uncertain and diminishing future, and their economic value to you will decline continually with each passing year. You can certainly help these individuals to think through their future on a more entrepreneurial basis, but until they actually become entrepreneurs, your ability to do business with them will decrease.

On the other hand, recognize that 99% of income growth and opportunities for life insurance agents over the next 25 years lies with clients who are entrepreneurs, and with the support personnel and families of these individuals.

Over the next quarter century, bureaucratic individuals will be on the defensive, searching for ways to maintain their existing security, status, and quality of life in the face of economic forces that are destructive to bureaucracy. Over this same period of time, entrepreneurial individuals will be on the offensive, searching for ways to maximize their opportunities, their capabilities, and their enhanced quality of life — and taking advantage of economic forces that favor entrepreneurism.

Strategy 5

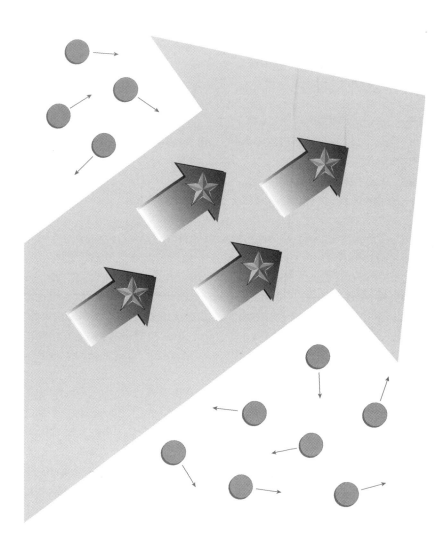

• **Focus your marketing strategies, resources, and talents on the entrepreneurial client base.**

Every dollar spent on an entrepreneurial client or prospect, in terms of return on investment, is worth 10 times the dollar spent on a bureaucratic individual. The same is true of time; every hour of your time spent with an entrepreneurial individual is 10 times more productive than an hour spent with a bureaucratic client or prospect. And every entrepreneurial relationship is 10 times more likely to lead to high quality referrals that offer the possibility of even greater return on investment.

Entrepreneurs, because they are in control of their own money, their own time, and their own organizations, are able to make decisions much more quickly, implement solutions more strategically, and commit themselves to a much longer period of planning.

Focus on the entrepreneurs.

• **Grow into the future through the constant acquisition of grateful entrepreneurial clients.**

For all the opportunities that are open to entrepreneurs, their lives are not easy. This will be even more the case as the global economy becomes more unpredictable.

The average entrepreneurial business owner is frequently overachieving, overworked, worried about competition, burdened with too many details and roles, guilty about poor quality of life, and dangerously underprotected in the critical areas of personal and company finances. They are frequently lonely, feel misunderstood, and are reluctant to give up control to those who want to support them.

Above all, most entrepreneurs are poorly advised.

The life insurance agent who becomes an expert at solving the problems and assisting with the solutions of the entrepreneurial individual also acquires a lifelong friend.

If you develop a growing network of dozens and hundreds of clients like this, these lifelong friends will do all of your marketing for you over the remainder of your career.

Strategy 6

Focus On The Biggest Cheque, And Organize Everything Around It

Strategy 6

Focus On The Biggest Cheque, And Organize Everything Around It

Ninety-five percent of insurance agents shy away from asking for premium cheques much larger than $5,000 per year. There are two main reasons for this reluctance:

One, above $5,000, the client's accountant usually gets involved in the buying decision, and many agents don't like dealing with accountants (or lawyers).

Two, the agent's product knowledge, marketing habits, support structure, and client market are geared to below $5,000 prospects.

Consequently, most agents find themselves boxed into low-level results, with little confidence, ability, or opportunity to go to a higher market. As the years go by, an agent with low premium cases will acquire hundreds if not thousands of small clients, all of whom require just as much servicing work as larger clients.

And the vast majority of the referrals from this client base tend to be the same — individuals with low premium policies.

The top agents operate in an opposite fashion: they continually train themselves to ask for and receive larger premium cheques. In fact, they use the device of asking for "the largest cheque" as one of their main impetuses for improving every aspect of their insurance practice.

The 21ˢᵗ Century Agent, therefore, will continually transform his or her practice to achieve larger premium cheques — which causes a never-ending improvement of knowledge, skills, habits, and support structures, and a constant upgrading of the client base.

Again, this cuts against the grain of the way that agents are trained to think and operate within the career agency system, where quantity of lives is more important than overall premium dollars (and commission dollars).

The following are the key components of this "largest cheque" strategy:

• Recognize that you may be stuck at a certain size of premium sale.

There's a quick way to determine where your present level of confidence is in relation to premium dollars. Go back three years, and in each year list, and then average, your 10 biggest premium sales. Then average your averages for these three years.

The resulting figure will tell you the level of transaction that has become habitual for you. It will tell you how confident you are about your product knowledge, about your support structure, and about your referral network. More than that, it will tell you what your judgment is about your own abilities.

As a final exercise, compare this figure with the premium dollars that you are paying for your own insurance policies. There are a lot of agents who by their own low investments in themselves indicate that they do not really believe in life insurance, that they do not really believe in large premiums. So why should any of their prospects or clients?

• Establish a goal for consistently achieving cheques at a much higher premium level.

There's a general law concerning the human brain: we only notice those things that our brain considers important. *Our eyes only see, and our ears only hear, what our brain is looking for.*

If you are looking for a $5,000 premium cheque, your eyes and ears will pick up on the information necessary for that size of sale. If

Strategy 6

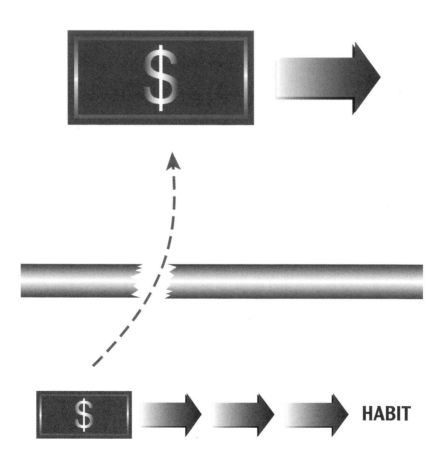

HABIT

you are looking for a $50,000 premium cheque, your eyes and ears will pick up all the information needed for that result.

Your analysis of the 10 biggest cheques for the past three years may reveal that you are stuck at the $5,000 level. So, in order to break through this level, establish a goal for $10,000 for the end of this year, $15,000 for next year, and $25,000 for the year after.

As soon as you do this, you will begin to experience a subtle transformation of your entire approach to marketing insurance. Your product knowledge will increase. You will develop new abilities. You will begin upgrading your support staff. And you will begin meeting and being introduced to higher quality prospects.

All because your brain is focused on the largest cheque.

• Gear all progress and growth within your business to the next highest cheque.

At any given time over the remaining years of your insurance career, you can be training yourself to achieve the next "largest cheque." As soon as you become confident and consistent at one level, set your sights on a higher level of premium sales.

Through this deceptively simple exercise, you will continually upgrade your client relationships, deepen your product knowledge, improve your support system, and focus all your work habits to support a high level of performance.

Whether they are conscious of this largest cheque strategy or not, this is how the top life insurance agents have always leveraged themselves into extraordinary resources and capabilities, larger sales, and bigger opportunities.

Strategy 7

Focus On Exclusive Standards, And Reject The Non-Qualifiers

Strategy 7

Focus On Exclusive Standards, And Reject The Non-Qualifiers

Warren Buffet, one of the most successful investors in the world, has three preliminary standards for judging his opportunities, he never deals with anyone that he does not (1) *trust,* (2) *respect,* and (3) *like* — regardless of how good the numbers look.

The most successful life insurance agents use similar standards for screening their prospects and judging their clients. There are only certain kinds of individuals that they are willing to work with, and they stick to these standards, even at the cost of bypassing what may look like big opportunities.

The key here is to work only with individuals with whom you can have a long-term, mutually satisfying, and beneficial relationship.

The 21ˢᵗ Century Agent realizes that the overall quality of his or her practice stems directly from establishing, communicating, and adhering to a set of high standards and personal ground rules for every aspect of his or her business.

• Recognize that you need to do business with only a very small part of the population.

In the scheme of things, a successful agent needs to deal with, at most, only 200 to 300 high quality clients in the course of a career.

From each of these individuals will come anywhere from six to 10 high quality sales, either directly or by way of referrals.

A high quality client, by our definition, is an entrepreneur with constantly increasing goals, capabilities, and opportunities who also has a multitude of interests and commitments outside of business.

This is a man or woman who has found a unique niche in an expanding marketplace and who has learned how to take advantage of the changes caused by microtechnology. He or she is someone whose attitudes, ambitions, business strategies, and overall lifestyle are in tune with the major trends of the 21ˢᵗ century.

This is a person of the future, rather than the past.

From the standpoint of personal qualities, the high quality client is a giver rather than a taker. He or she does not live off the system but, rather, creates new systems that provide opportunities for hundreds and thousands of other people.

This is someone who lives by the two entrepreneurial decisions: depend upon your own ability for financial security and never expect opportunity unless you first create value.

We are now in an historical period where hundreds of thousands of individuals like this are emerging each year, responding to the opportunities that are being created by the laws of the microchip.

• Create your own "rules of the game" that define exactly how you want to operate into the future.

Many life insurance agents are willing to work with anyone who can write a premium checque. Since they'll deal with anyone and anything, that's what they end up getting. As a result, they feel forced to put up with all kinds of client demands that are annoying, frustrating, distracting, and exhausting. They have told their clients in one way or another that they are available at any hour of the day, any day of the year — and so clients take them up on the offer.

And then these agents wonder why after 10 years in the business their lives have become so complicated and unfulfilling. At this point they invari-

Strategy 7

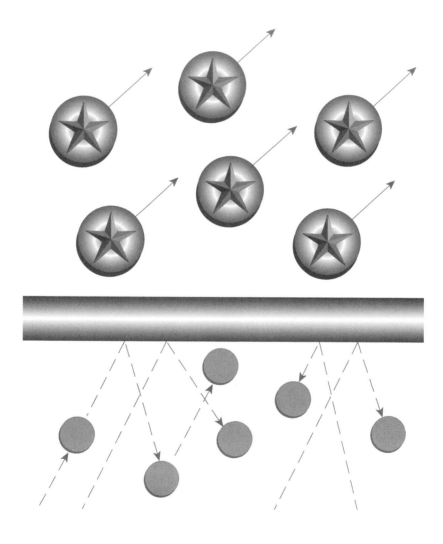

ably begin to blame the industry, their insurance companies, their support staff, and their clients for all the confusion and chaos in their lives.

But this whole mess is entirely of their own making; they never told the world how they wanted to do business.

Simplicity and fulfillment in life, not to mention success, come from having clearly stated ground rules and sticking to them. This means, first of all, stating to yourself exactly how you want to operate your business over the remaining years of your career.

Here's an exercise to clarify your "rules of the game." Using a large artist's pad, spend an afternoon writing and diagramming how you want to operate in every situation related to your business for the rest of your career. This will include when you want to work, your vacations and free days, your income and savings, what kind of clients and prospects you want, where you want to meet with them, and how you want to be supported in every area of your work.

Then have it typed for a set of rules which you review and strengthen on a quarterly basis. After a year of doing this, you will be amazed at how your life has been simplified and made more enjoyable in the process. You will also notice that you have better clients and a higher income.

• Communicate your standards to everyone who matters.

Once your rules of the game are clear to you, then make them clear to everyone else whose actions affect your performance and success. This list should include your family, your friends, your support staff, your advisors and suppliers, your centers of influence, your clients, and every new prospect that you meet.

You will be amazed at how many people will respond positively and supportively. Those who don't will quickly leave your life.

Strategy 8

Focus On Client Advisors, And Multiply The Marketing Network

Strategy 8

Focus On Client Advisors, And Multiply The Marketing Network

The bigger the insurance sales opportunity, the more certain that an accountant and/or lawyer will be involved in the process. For many agents, this is a negative. The client's advisors are seen as adversaries, as threats, and as sales preventers.

But the knowledge revolution caused by microtechnology is destroying much of the lucrative boilerplate services in both the accounting and legal industries. This is forcing accountants and lawyers to be more entrepreneurial, and many are establishing strategic alliances with other specialists, including top insurance agents, as a way of increasing creative services to their clients.

The 21ˢᵗ Century Agent will master the large case market by using accountants and lawyers as the primary marketing network for developing endless opportunities.

Like all other professions, accounting and law over the past 60 years have become increasingly bureaucratic. This occurred for two reasons. One, because the biggest and best-paying clients were large bureaucratic organizations, especially corporations. Two, because the biggest accounting and legal firms became huge bureaucracies themselves. Enormous status was attached both to being a partner in these big firms and to having prestigious bureaucratic clients.

That is no longer the case. From being the kings of the mountain in bureaucratic society, the accounting and legal professions have fallen in stature over the past two decades to being just two more specialties in a vast, highly competitive knowledge economy where success for all specialties now depends on microtechnology, creative marketing, proactive problem solving, and value-added service.

All of which makes the smartest accountants and lawyers more open to forming strategic alliances with top life insurance agents. As an agent, there are several things to think about:

• **Recognize that all accounting and legal advisors to your clients must also operate as entrepreneurs.**

Twenty years ago, billable hours for accountants and lawyers was a wonderful, lucrative concept. But in the 1990s the concept of billable hours is a trap, a barrier to creativity, and a barrier to increased income.

It doesn't matter how much an accountant or lawyer charges per hour, even if it's $500; there's still an upper limit to how much he or she can make. In the knowledge economy, most accountants and lawyers are like highly paid factory workers, and many of them are realizing this.

If you get paid by the hour, then you don't get paid for results, which is where the really big money is. In order to get paid for results, you have to give up the billable hours, and this is what scares many accountants and lawyers today. They don't know if they're good enough to make a living based purely on results.

You, as a life insurance agent, someone who has lived your entire professional career getting paid only for results, are in a position to show accountants and lawyers how they can make a transition to a results-based profession. In making this crossover, they will become increasingly entrepreneurial in their outlook and performance and will see you as a valuable advisor and ally.

Strategy 8

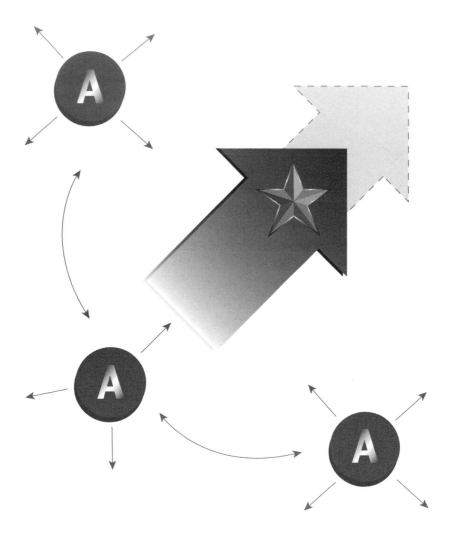

- **Create opportunities for advisors to be heroes, and multiply their income.**

Because many traditional ways of billing clients are disappearing for lawyers and accountants, you have an opportunity to show new ways for advisors to assist their clients.

Life insurance in its many forms is one of the most remarkable financial inventions, right up there with compound interest. In virtually every successful plan for long-range wealth creation under today's tax laws, life insurance is probably the most crucial instrument, yet most accounting and legal advisors are unaware of the specific benefits and solutions.

Position yourself as the insurance expert to all the accountants and lawyers who advise your insurance prospects and clients. Think of the client situation from the advisors' standpoint. Design solutions for the clients that make the accountants and lawyers look like heroes, solutions that increase their income opportunities, even if it's only more billable hours.

As long as you're willing to let the advisors have the credit, you will always get the commissions and further opportunities.

- **Establish a process where advisors are eager to market you to their other clients.**

The agents who make Top Of The Table every year all share the same marketing strategy — they use top accountants and lawyers as their main sales force. Over the next 25 years, you can make your marketing activities simple, predictable, and productive by aligning your best insurance solutions with the most important needs of the other professionals who advise your prospects and clients. Help these advisors to solidify and expand their client relationships, and they will be eager to introduce you to their other clients.

Think about this possibility: Twenty highly influential accountants and lawyers working on your behalf, introducing you to 100 highly qualified situations every year for the rest of your career. And all you have to do is help them become more entrepreneurial, look like heroes to their clients, and achieve greater income.

Strategy 9

Focus On Future-Based Clients, And Delegate Past-Based Clients

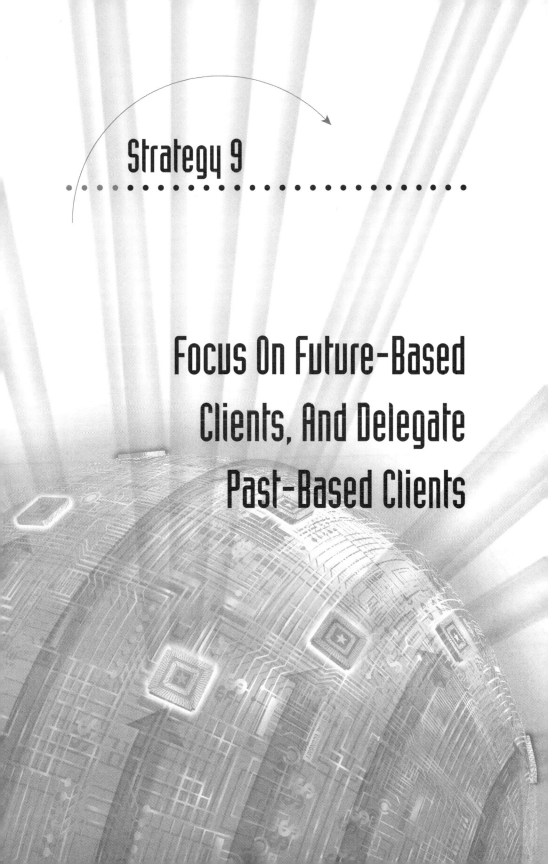

Strategy 9

Focus On Future-Based Clients, And Delegate Past-Based Clients

Some life insurance prospects may have big estates and companies, but they don't have big futures. Their growth and achievement is in the past; their lives have run out of energy. This is the main reason why many private companies and personal estates fail to survive beyond the first generation: there are no further dreams, goals, vision, or future.

A person without dreams, no matter what age and no matter how successful and wealthy, is essentially a dead-end prospect. He or she is usually very difficult to deal with, resistant to decision making, unresponsive to a big perspective, and suspicious of creative solutions.

Yet because of the prospect's high net worth statement, a lot of life insurance agents get seduced into situations like this. They devote an inordinate amount of time, attention, and emotional energy to a single case because they see it as a "huge opportunity."

A huge opportunity like this can ruin an agent's year. Five of them can sidetrack or ruin a career.

On the other hand, there are highly successful individuals who never stop growing and achieving. No matter how successful their past, no matter how powerful their present status, their future is always bigger and more exciting to them and those around them.

The 21ˢᵗ Century Agent, therefore, will continually be surrounded by 30 to 40 relationships with individuals who are always powerfully motivated by a future that will always be in need of increased insurance underwriting.

One of the most important skills that a life agent can develop is to detect immediately whether a prospect or client is "past-based" or "future-based." There are several aspects to distinguishing one kind of person from the other:

• Recognize that some insurance prospects and clients have decided to stop growing.
Despite having sold life insurance for many years, many agents really don't grasp the significance of this fact — *life insurance is a totally future-based concept and product.*
In other words, the need for insurance is something that must first be created in the imagination of the prospect and client. They have to see something important about their lives that has not yet happened. There has to be something at risk in their mind's eye that is bigger, and better, and different from what they have now.
If a person has decided to stop growing, his or her future will appear no different than the present. There will be no emotional commitment to something bigger and better. This is the biggest reason why most people are underinsured and will stay underinsured until it is too late — because mentally, emotionally, and imaginatively they have stopped growing. Therefore, the first thing to determine in any sales situation is whether the prospect or client is still growing. If not, then move on quickly to someone else, someone who is future-based.

• Ask every prospect and client what has to happen over the next three years.
For a life agent, the most important and powerful question to ask prospects and existing clients is: *"If we were meeting here three years from today, and you were looking back over those three years, what has to have happened for you to feel happy with your progress."*

Strategy 9

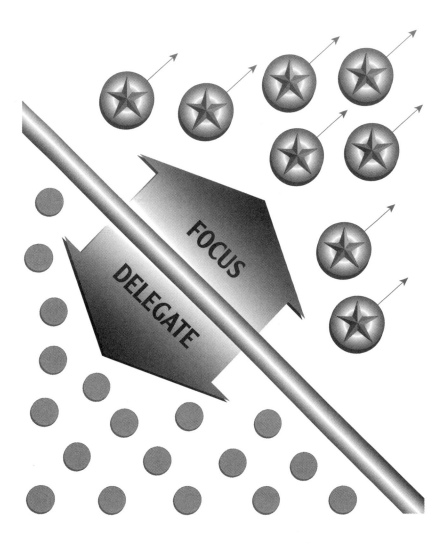

The past-based individual will give a short, vague, indefinite, unenthusiastic answer to this question. There will be very few details, no emotion, and nothing exciting.

The future-based individual, on the other hand, will give you a list of specific goals, each of which represents a significant improvement over the present situation, each of which is stimulating, and each of which will require growth on his or her part. As the future-based person is answering the question, he or she will become more and more emotionally committed to the future, and will become motivated to take some kind of immediate action.

The past-based person's answer is a dead end and should be seen by an agent as a stop sign. The future-based person's answer is a wide gateway to an exciting relationship over many years, and an opportunity for significant life insurance underwriting.

• Focus at any given time on 30 to 40 big futures as the foundation for all future opportunities.

Probably the biggest obstacle to any life insurance agent's career development is being in the company of prospects and clients who have chosen not to grow any further.

On the other hand, the biggest boost to a career is to be continually in the company of 30 to 40 prospects and clients with "big futures." As an agent, your future success is tied directly to one continuous process of identifying where the big futures are, helping these future-based individuals to clarify the specific goals that make up their vision, and then assisting them to achieve those goals.

Some of the solutions in these "big futures" will require life insurance; many of them will not. But if you help your future-based prospects and clients with their goals, they will continually create new opportunities for you to sell more life insurance.

Use the three-year question to filter out the non-growth individuals from your prospect list and client base. Then clarify the three-year plans that the future-based people provide to you — and continually use these plans as the basis for developing all sales opportunities over the remaining course of your career.

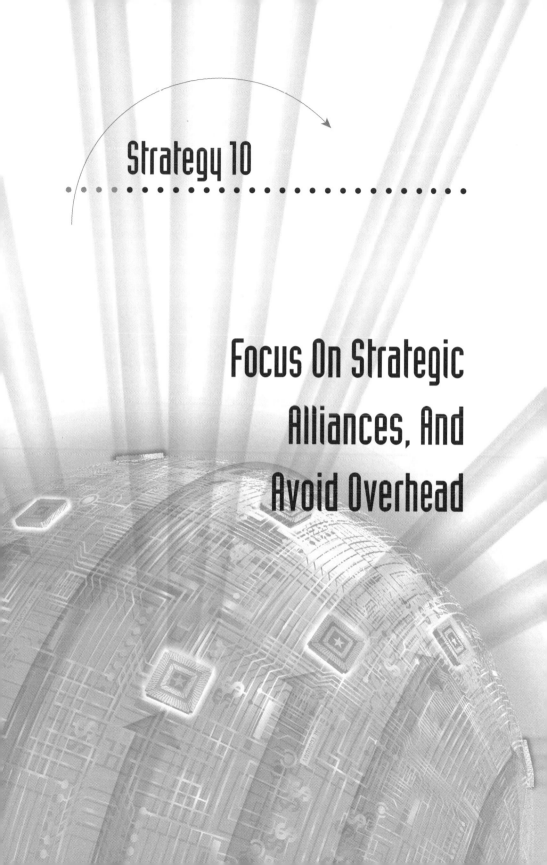

Strategy 10

Focus On Strategic Alliances, And Avoid Overhead

Strategy 10

Focus On Strategic Alliances, And Avoid Overhead

As the marketplace for all services becomes more entrepreneurial, the most successful business practitioners are acquiring superb resources and capabilities without adding to the cost of overhead.

The secret lies in strategic alliances, for example, between skilled life insurance agents and equally skilled accountants, lawyers, compensation consultants, stock brokers, computer consultants, and software specialists, who all value and recommend each other's services.

Within the insurance industry itself, life agents are specializing in one particular area, e.g., retirement planning or charitable trusts, and referring other business to equally skilled specialists in other insurance areas.

In a world governed by specialized knowledge, the 21st Century Agent will become a superb specialist — and depend on strategic alliances with other specialists to provide a full range of services to clients.

The famous expert on organizational management, Peter Drucker, says that in the global knowledge economy of the 21st century, every person regardless of his or her occupation, will be a "knowledge worker." From this standpoint, then, medical doctors are just knowledge workers as are lawyers, accountants, politicians, airline pilots, janitors, and insurance agents! Each of them possesses a specific kind of knowledge that, in order to be useful, must be integrated with the knowledge of other specialists into a larger system of decision and action.

Therefore, once a person grasps that virtually all solutions in the marketplace now require the integration of many different kinds of knowledge, involving the work of many different knowledge specialists, then all kinds of new teamwork and all kinds of new strategic alliances become possible, necessary, and profitable.

As a life insurance agent, there are several things to remember about working and thriving in the knowledge economy:

• Recognize that all the knowledge and capabilities you need can be available at little or no cost.

It is now possible, as never before, to develop great knowledge capabilities within your insurance practice — *without incurring a large overhead in the process.*

By the end of the 20ᵗʰ century, Peter Drucker also predicts that approximately 50% of all people in the work force will be self-employed — self-employed knowledge workers, all of whom will also want access to great knowledge capabilities, without incurring overhead.

This is a major global trend. This is a watershed in human history, when the global work population is reorganizing itself on the basis of infinitely shared knowledge at the lowest possible cost.

Therefore, it is possible as a life insurance agent to link up with dozens of other knowledge specialists and utilize their expertise without paying for it. All you have to do is create opportunities for these specialists to be paid by your clients, or pay for their expertise yourself, for very short, very strategic periods of time in such a way that the results pay for the costs many times over.

Strategy 10

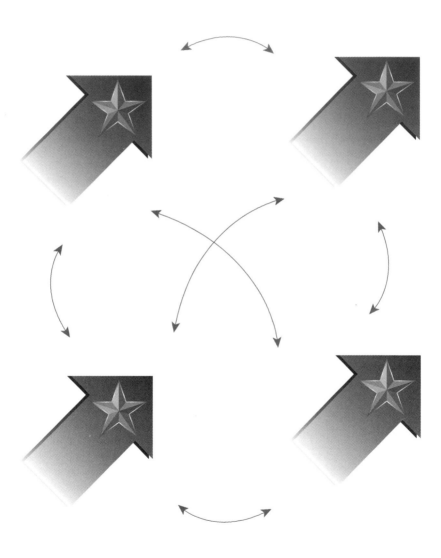

• **Create a network of strategic alliances to support and enhance every part of your business.**

Make a list today of the different kinds of expertise — that is, specialized knowledge — that you would like to have supporting your entire insurance practice.

Twenty years ago, if you wanted all that expertise, you would have hired it, put it on the payroll, made it part of a big overhead that gave you ulcers and kept you awake at night. A lot of insurance agents in the 1970s and 1980s, when they went independent, tried to form all-purpose agencies. They staffed up with lawyers, accountants, actuaries, group specialties, and dozens of support staff. It all added up to a huge overhead that killed profits, and turned the entrepreneurial agent into a bureaucratic manager.

In the 1990s, none of this is necessary. You can do an inventory of your knowledge needs, and then hire the specialists by the hour or by the project. Or, better still, you can joint venture with the other knowledge specialists so that they handle their part of specific projects, and you handle yours. Everybody on the team operates as an entrepreneur, and nobody takes on anyone else's overhead.

• **Create a resource network of problem solvers for your clients.**

After you've secured your own knowledge requirements, look at the kinds of specialized capabilities that your clients need to solve their problems and achieve their goals.

Going back to Strategy 9, and to the three-year plans that you will be compiling on all your growth clients, identify every knowledge resource that would be useful to your clients in achieving their plans.

Find the appropriate knowledge specialists and refer them to your clients as a value-added service. The knowledge specialists will thank you, and so will your clients. The other knowledge specialists will return the favor by referring your services to their clients.

Your clients will see you as one of the most useful people they have ever met — someone who is a master of the specialized knowledge economy of the 1990s. You're not just an insurance agent, but someone who can assist them with all their goals, both business and personal.

Strategy 11

Focus On Money-Making Activities, And Get Rid Of Your Office

Strategy 11

Focus On Money-Making Activities, And Get Rid Of Your Office

The word "bureaucracy" comes from the French language, meaning "the rule of the office." And offices, especially for life agents, are places filled with bureaucratic details and messes — all the "stuff" that prevents an agent from concentrating on the most important money-making activities.

Although there are obvious exceptions, most life insurance agents are least productive when in their offices. They become bogged down with endless paperwork and "stuff" that undermines their ability to sell.

The 21ˢᵗ Century Agent — through the use of sophisticated computer, telephone, and facsimile technologies — will significantly increase his or her productivity by not having a personal office.

Instead, he or she will operate out of an efficient meeting room that is completely free of paperwork or operate from home, from a cottage, or a boat — anywhere that he or she can meet with clients.

In The Strategic Coach Program, when it is first suggested to our clients that they get rid of their personal office and replace it with just a meeting room, many are horrified. Their office is like a security blanket. They can retreat into the inner sanctum, into their warm and cozy cocoon, close the door, and there — surrounded by their mountains of files, paper, magazines, and reports — nobody can watch what they're doing.

Whatever they're doing, it's a good guess that they're not making any money. It's a good guess they're not developing money-making ideas, or developing money-making relationships.

For many life insurance agents, their personal identity is tied to this piece of real estate, furniture, and equipment called the office. Give up their office! What would their clients think if they learned that the agent didn't have an office! What would staff think!

Chances are, your clients, if they're successful entrepreneurs, couldn't care less. They're too busy trying to be successful. And your support staff would like nothing better than to free you from all the mess and clutter that keeps you from bringing in the money that guarantees their paycheque.

In exploring the possibility of not having an office, here are some things to think about:

• Recognize that your most important activities are face-to-face communication.

When clients buy life insurance, they're not buying a policy, they're buying an agent. They're buying someone who looks and sounds like he or she knows the best thing for the client to do. They're buying someone who will take all their concerns into account and come up with a product that protects their future.

The life insurance sale, probably more than any other kind of sale in the marketplace, is based on human chemistry and trust. All of this requires maximum face-to-face communication, which can occur anywhere.

The most successful agents in the world are the ones who spend the most time in face-to-face meetings, and who spend the least time amount of time in their "office." The least successful agents, on the other hand, hide in their offices shuffling paper in order to avoid actual sales opportunities.

Strategy 11

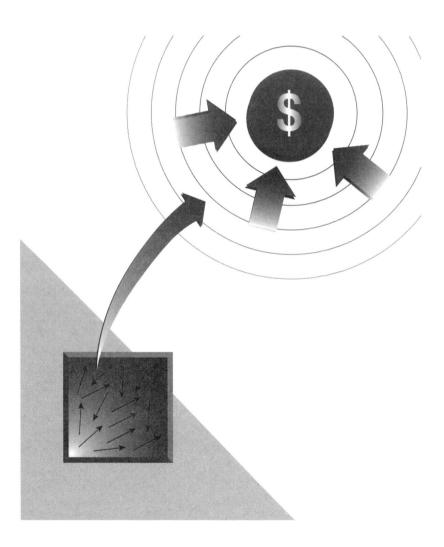

• Create a meeting and work space that is completely free of "stuff."

Move everything out of your existing office and replace your office furniture with a round conference table and four comfortable chairs. Remove all personal pictures, certificates, plaques, and other personal items. Replace them with high quality paintings, photographs, or other artwork.

Make sure there are outlets and phone jacks for using a computer and telephone when you're doing work on cases. The computer and phone equipment can be on a mobile station that can be rolled out of the meeting room when you're not using it.

Here are the ground rules: the meeting room is completely free from all "stuff" and "messes" at the end of each business day. No paper of any kind comes into the room except what you are going to be working on that day. When you stop working on a project, it immediately goes back to a support person's office.

Pull this off, and from this one change you'll see your income jump by 25% in the first 12 months.

• Go to the office only when there is money to be made.

The "no office" strategy has one purpose: to focus all your attention on money-making activities without any distractions. Without an office, and the clutter and distractions that come along with it, you have no alternative except to meet with prospects and clients and sell.

If there is no one to meet, if there is no important casework to complete, then don't go to your place of business. Use your cellular phone and laptop computer from your car. Invite someone to breakfast, lunch, or dinner. Go to the club, a game, a concert, or to the theater. Go fishing or play golf. Any of these activities is far more likely to lead to an insurance sale than sitting in your office.

Once you get rid of your office, you will begin to see your business strictly in terms of an *activity,* where you try to make money, rather than as a *place,* where you try to look busy.

Strategy 12

Focus On Staff
Capabilities, And Give Up
Control Of "Stuff"

Strategy 12

Focus On Staff Capabilities, And Give Up Control Of "Stuff"

The biggest obstacle to a life insurance agent's advancement as an entrepreneur is the unwillingness and/or inability to delegate the "stuff" that prevents the agent from focusing on his or her most important money-making activities and relationships. The reason for this failure is not a lack of competent staff but the need of the agent to control all the details of his or her practice.

On the other hand, highly successful entrepreneurs in all fields give up control of how things get done. They see themselves as performers who must be freed up from everything except the most important economic activities.

The 21st Century Agent will continually delegate to superb support staff, thereby freeing all work time to concentrate on the two or three most important sales activities.

The most successful delegation models are in entertainment and sports. A top entertainer like Frank Sinatra, for example, or a sports superstar like Michael Jordan, doesn't do anything in his business except perform. Frank Sinatra does not move pianos, and Michael Jordan doesn't sweep the basketball floor. In each case, there is a superb support team or system that handles all the details. This is very clear in entertainment and sports, but it's just as true everywhere else. When performers in any field can just perform, they bring in big dollars, which pays for a great support system.

Which brings us to the business of life insurance and your performance as an agent. When you can focus all your time, attention, and expertise on just selling, solving problems, and making money, there's no upper limit to the amount of money you can make.

In order to achieve this, you have to keep several things in mind:

• Recognize that your most important asset is your creative focus time.
Here's an exercise for you. Think ahead over the next three months and establish an income goal. With that in mind, identify the one activity that is going to be most crucial in achieving that goal. Then, the second most crucial activity. And then, the third.

Now examine these three activities that you've chosen as the most crucial. Do they involve creativity? Do they make use of your best abilities? Do they involve your best relationships and opportunities? The answer, naturally, is yes to all three questions.

So why don't you do just these three activities all the time, and delegate everything else to skilled support people? This is what Frank Sinatra has done for the past fifty years. Your creative focus time — filled with your three most important activities — is the single most important asset in your business. You should do everything in your power to protect this time and continually expand it.

• Surround yourself with individuals who are strong where you are weak.
A lot of people take some very bad advice when they are six years old and never recover for the rest of their lives. Somebody tells them that "the secret to success in life is to work on your weaknesses" and they believe it.

Strategy 12

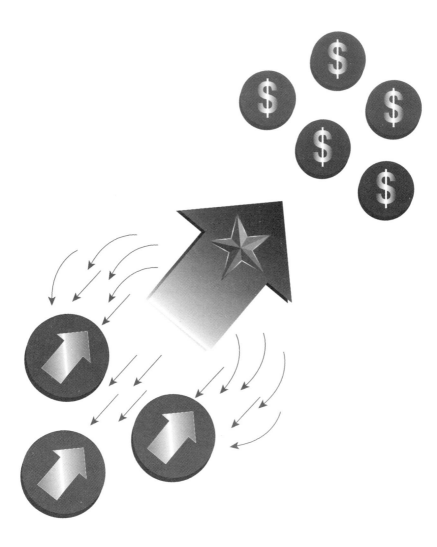

Here's all you need to know about this philosophy — if you spend your whole life working on your weaknesses, by the end of your life, you'll have a lot of really strong weaknesses.

The truth is just the opposite. *The secret to success in life is to focus entirely on your strengths, and delegate your weaknesses to highly skilled people who are strong where you are weak.* Most successful life insurance agents are good at one thing: they have a unique ability to give their clients the confidence to identify and make crucial financial decisions which affect the clients' whole lifetime. Period. That's it. There isn't anything else a life insurance agent is really good at. Everything else in the insurance practice — all the details, all the preparation, all the follow-through, coordination, and implementation — can be done by skilled support people.

• Create job descriptions that free you from all activities that do not make money.

Here's another exercise. Write your three most important money-making activities in the middle of a sheet of paper. Then draw a circle around these items. Now, outside the circle divide the rest of the page into eight parts by drawing spokes out from the circle to the edge of the page. In each of the parts, write one specific activity that you are now doing that interferes with your ability to focus on the three activities in the center. Go around the circle and list eight activities — in your business or personal life — that interfere with your focus activities and time. As you are doing this, you may notice that your stress level goes down. That's because all the eight activities that you are listing rob you of energy and cause you frustration.

Use these eight items as the basis for designing the job descriptions that will totally support your money-making activities. Then start the process of putting the right people in the right jobs.

Every 90 days, take a look at the circle. Keep refining your description of your own three activities and keep adding greater detail to the job descriptions that you need to support you.

In just six months, you'll be amazed at the difference this makes to your confidence, your performance, and your results.

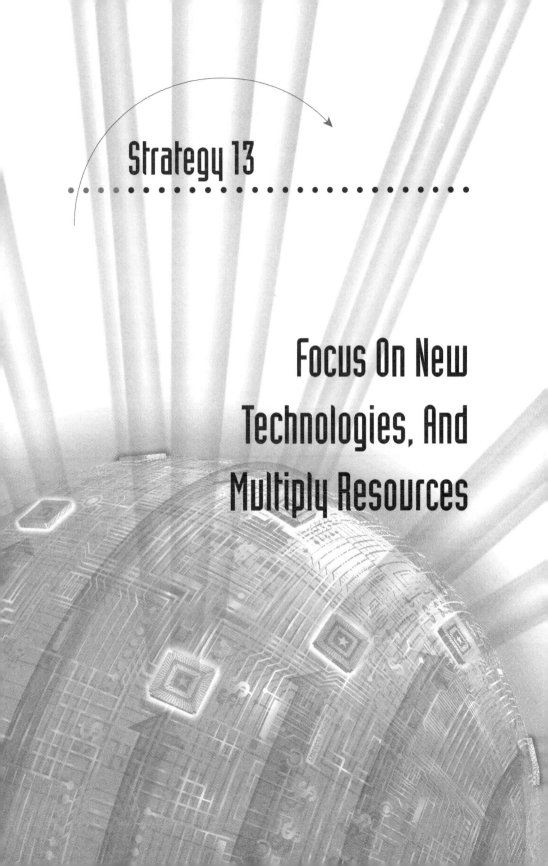

Strategy 13

Focus On New Technologies, And Multiply Resources

Strategy 13

Focus On New Technologies, And Multiply Resources

Pilzer's formula, W = R x T, *wealth equals existing resources multi- plied by new technologies*, becomes a fundamental strategy for all entrepreneurs in the 1990s to increase the income of their businesses without adding bureaucracy. For entrepreneurial life insurance agents, this means utilizing appropriate microchip-based technologies to mul- tiply the value of existing staff, existing products, existing clients, and existing referral opportunities.

We are entering an age where a single agent, supported by three or four skilled staff members, and equipped with microchip technolo- gies in all areas of the practice, will be able to outproduce a bureau- cratic organization with 50 managers and workers.

The 21st Century Agent will see technology as a constant future multiplier of his or her management and marketing capabilities and will keep current with the latest breakthroughs that can enhance his or her productivity.

We have become in the 20th century so accustomed to technologi- cal breakthroughs that many of us take them for granted. But there's real magic at work here. No fairy tale has wonders greater than those produced by the microchip in the world over the past 25 years. Wherever we turn, microchips are making things better, faster, and smarter.

In order to make your insurance practice better, faster, and smarter, it's necessary to utilize technology in a *strategic* manner. Here are some guidelines:

• **Recognize that your most important resources are focus activities — yours and those of your team.**

Technology cannot really multiply your existing resources until you first know what those resources are. There is an easy way to determine this. Simply identify the three most important activities of each person in your team.

For starters, you are a resource. Think back to the three most important money-making activities that you identified in Strategy 12. The focus time that you can devote to these three activities is the single most important resource in your company.

How can you apply new technologies to each one of these activities in such a way that it multiplies your effectiveness? How would a computer help? What about new software? Spend an hour thinking about these and other possibilities, and you're sure to come up with three or four ideas that can be implemented within the next 90 days.

There will be immediate payoffs in terms of your income, and especially in terms of your personal confidence. Each improvement that you make will encourage you to make even more.

• **Conduct a regular technology review, make strategic improvements, and maintain a technology file.**

After multiplying the effectiveness of your own focus activities, do the same thing for each of your support staff. What are each person's three most important activities, and how can they be multiplied through technology?

If you have three support staff, there are likely 6 to 10 improvements that you can make using technology over the next 12 months. There is no need to analyze the situation any further, because unless a

Strategy 13

new technology multiplies your crucial activities, and those of your staff, it's not worth bringing it into your business. A lot of entrepreneurs fall in love with technology without clearly thinking through how it will affect the overall team. In such a situation, technology can cause problems rather than solutions.

Just remember that all your other resources — products, services, clients, centers of influence, knowledge, information, suppliers, and strategic alliances — are simply extensions of your activities and those of your support team. Every 90 days, conduct a "technology review" based on the process above. Each person reports what progress has been made, what further progress can be achieved over the next quarter, and what specific actions need to be taken.

It's also important to have a "technology file" of new ideas that you pick up from magazines, newspapers, or from technology vendors. The important thing to remember here is that it is the effectiveness of your activities that is important, not the technologies themselves.

• Use the Six Laws of the Microchip as a guide for developing technological confidence.

Trend 2 outlines a new structure of human development and progress based on the extraordinary evolution of the microchip.

Some life insurance agents are going to recognize this new reality and use it as a source of endless opportunity over the course of their career. Others are going to ignore it until they are forced to change in ways that they dislike and are not prepared for.

We live in a world where technology develops incessantly according to its own internal laws. Very few people have an overview of this process, and no one is in control of its direction. We can learn to adapt to technological evolution, but we cannot stop it or alter its course.

Here's a way for you to keep adapting — at the end of each 90 days, when you conduct your technology review, also read the Six Laws and reflect on how you are aligning your progress with the forces of technology. Your analyses, decisions, strategies, and improvements will continually give you great *technological confidence.*

Strategy 14

Focus On Superb Communication, And Delegate The Technicalities

Strategy 14

Focus On Superb Communication, And Delegate The Technicalities

Life insurance agents do not get paid to do technical work; that's for technicians. The technical work (the number crunching, the research, and the packaging) is important to back up a sales presentation, but that's not what determines the sale.

The best agents get paid for doing only two things:

One, helping highly successful clients to be clear and excited about their personal futures.

Two, enabling these individuals to make strategic decisions that are crucial to their future well-being and peace of mind.

Both these abilities require superb communication skills, which means the ability to ask insightful questions, the ability to be a great listener, the ability to synthesize crucial issues, and the ability to present clear-cut strategies.

A great communicator with a one-page presentation will always outsell a poor communicator with 200 pages of exhaustive research.

The 21st Century Agent will focus his or her greatest skill development on understanding how clients and prospects look at the future — and then using the work of superb technicians to create underwriting solutions for those futures.

Great communication for a life insurance agent must be based on the three fundamental principles of honesty, clarity, and confidence.

Honesty means that you're not trying to present yourself as something you're not.

Clarity means that you're talking about what the other person is interested in, what the other person's world is all about.

Confidence means that no particular sales situation is that crucial to you. You are totally confident that you have an extraordinary product and service to provide to the right 100 people every year; it's just a matter of helping them become committed to the future that they really want to have.

To develop a greater sense of honesty, clarity, and confidence, here are some important factors to keep in mind:

• **Recognize that you are already a better communicator than 99% of the population.**

The ability to sell anything is a very high form of communication. Of all the products sold on this planet, life insurance is probably the toughest to sell, and you've already proven that you do this extremely well.

Life insurance is such a tough product for most people to sell because it is not a product that people can touch, taste, see, or smell. It is a "product *of* the mind," a "product *in* the mind," and a "product *for* the mind." In other words, life insurance is entirely a product of the creative imagination, and entirely a product of creative communication.

That is why, as an agent, you should focus much of your personal development on becoming an even greater communicator. You should constantly be developing new ways of presenting the extraordinary benefits of life insurance to the creative imaginations of your prospects and clients. Once you engage them there, once they are convinced and committed on that level, the technicalities are just a way of wrapping up the sale.

Strategy 14

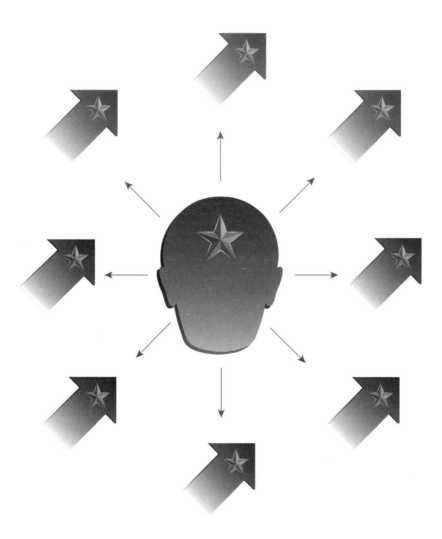

- **Commit yourself to just three benefit statements for the rest of your career.**

The biggest thing that kills good communication is the attempt to be all things to all people, which leads to dishonesty, lack of clarity, and low confidence. Right now, based on who you are and what your experience has been, there are only certain kinds of people that you should ever be selling to. And with this select group of prospects and clients, there are only certain things that you should be doing for them. In fact, no more than three things.

Here's the key to powerful communication that will last for your entire career — identify just three benefits that you would like to provide to your 10 best clients over the next 25 years. Then test yourself with this question: "If these three benefits were all I ever provided in my entire insurance career, would that be stimulating, satisfying, and fulfilling?"

When you find three benefits that you are totally committed to, then you can be sure that they will also be benefits that your clients, your centers of influence, and your support team will be committed to.

- **Build your entire organization around the communication and delivery of these three benefits.**

With total commitment to the three benefits, you can build your whole insurance business on the continual communication of these benefits.

The first step is in the hiring and training of your support team. Are these the kinds of individuals who represent your benefits? There has to be a total congruity between your message and your people.

Second, does every team member understand the benefits clearly? The entire purpose of all their work, day in and day out, is simply the delivery and reinforcement of these benefits to your clients.

Finally, does every improvement that you make to your business reinforce the communication of your three benefits? Don't make any changes, don't do anything new or different, unless it serves to further your fundamental value in the marketplace.

Strategy 15

Focus On Your Personal Wealth, And Avoid Cash Flow Pressures

Strategy 15

Focus On Your Personal Wealth, And Avoid Cash Flow Pressures

Many life insurance agents, in giving financial advice to their clients, are hypocrites simply because they themselves are poor managers of money. They try to sell strategies for wealth creation when they have accumulated very little wealth themselves.

This creates two negative psychological conditions in the agent.

One, a lack of integrity that invariably comes from not practicing what one preaches. This lack of integrity will betray itself in sales situations with prospects and clients who are good money managers.

Two, a state of anxiety about every sales situation, where the agent's own financial pressures take precedence over the client's best interests.

In order to establish and maintain a sense of financial integrity in all sales situations, an agent's own financial affairs must be solid.

The 21st Century Agent will focus on building his or her personal wealth and skills for financial management, thereby allowing him or her to deal with even the wealthiest clients in an experienced, confident, and knowledgable fashion.

Several years back, we asked a Top of the Table agent how his previous sales year had turned out. "Good news and bad news," he replied. "The good news is that it was the best year I've ever had. The bad news is that it had to be!"

Here is an individual who had made more than $1 million in pre-tax personal income, yet at the end of the year, he had nothing to show for it. "I'm always underdeposited at the bank," is how he put it.

There are a lot of successful agents who could echo his comments. They've earned six- and seven-figure incomes for 10 to 20 years, yet their net worth statements do not reflect this achievement. They've made a lot of money, yet they don't have a lot of money.

This squandering cannot help but adversely impact on the agent's business performance. Somewhere along the line, the lack of good financial management becomes a barrier to professional growth, no matter how talented the agent. It eats into concentration and confidence. It makes the agent dependent on the bank and the insurance companies, and it undermines the individual's credibility with support staff, centers of influence, and ultimately with clients.

By the same token, there are many other top agents who are held up as superb role models by everyone who knows them. They totally practice what they are preaching. They walk their talk. Everyone notices this and everyone is delighted to refer them to the best opportunities.

In your efforts to become this kind of role model, keep the following points in mind:

• Put yourself and your affairs in the hands of top financial consultants.

Jack Nicklaus has a golf coach, and Pavarotti has a singing coach. Just because you're a skilled life insurance agent doesn't mean that you can handle your own finances. Doctors don't operate on themselves, nor do dentists. And neither should you, as a financial specialist, be operating on your own finances.

In order to be a teacher in any field, you have to be teachable, which means that you should allow a top financial consultant to assist you in the same way that you assist your clients. Besides, the thing that you're really good at is selling, not managing, not investing, and

Strategy 15

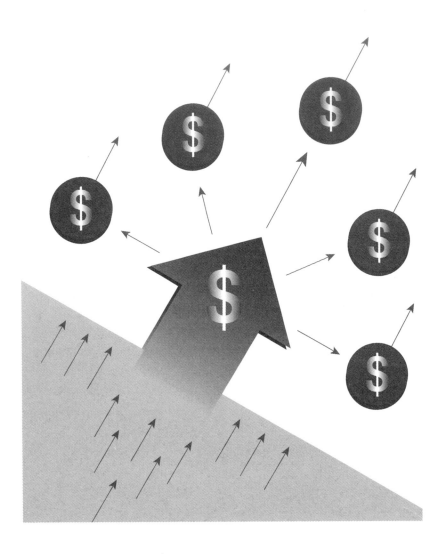

not keeping books. As part of your financial management structure, you should have yourself put on a budget and on a regular salary, with all other surplus income going into systematic savings and investment plans.

• Create a "walk-away fund" that enables you to walk away from any situation you don't like.

As a salesperson, you are at your most powerful and convincing when you don't need the sale — or the deal, in the case of your relationships with insurance companies.

In order to achieve this feeling of confidence in all selling and negotiating situations, create for yourself a "walk-away fund," which is a sum of money large enough for you to be able to walk away from any situation or relationship that you don't like.

How much money should be in this fund? You're the only one who can answer this question, but it should be a sufficient amount for you to feel relaxed about taking a pass on what other successful agents might see as a "huge opportunity." As a mental exercise, think of what $1 million in your walk-away fund would do for your selling and negotiating confidence right now.

• Communicate to everyone that you sell insurance for the love of the activity, not for the money.

Everyone loves buying from an agent who loves selling, and who loves what is being sold.

There are a lot of top life insurance agents who sell only because the money is good, and they need the money. They really don't like the business, and they wish they did something else. Everyone they meet, especially prospects, picks up on this negative attitude.

Here's a challenge then — over the next five years, make and save so much money that, if you chose, you wouldn't have to sell another insurance policy in your life. Then decide whether or not you love the business. Because at that point, if you discover that you really do love it, you will become an absolutely irresistible salesperson.

Strategy 16

Focus On Results, And Minimize Time And Effort

Strategy 16

There are two economies on the planet: first, the "time and effort" economy, which consists of jobs with a guaranteed income. Most people work in this economy because security is more important to them than opportunity.

Second, the "results" economy, made up of the entrepreneurs, in which there is no guaranteed income. Individuals choose to operate in this economy because opportunity is more important to them than security.

Life insurance agents are in the results economy, but most of them still operate according to the values of the time and effort economy.

The 21st Century Agent will focus on achieving ever higher results while continually minimizing the time and effort needed to achieve those results.

In The Strategic Coach Program, we tell this story to get across the difference between the results economy and the time and effort economy.

It's called the Jose Canseco Formula. Mr. Canseco, the famous home run hitter, signed a contract several years back for approximately $4.7 million per year. Now, what exactly does he do to deserve that kind of money? Well, he's not the greatest fielder or base runner, and he doesn't hit for a high average, so it must be the home runs. An average of 40 a year, when he's healthy.

Let's look at how he earns his $4.7 million. In a full season, he plays 162 games, during which he goes to bat approximately 700 times. Each time he goes to bat, he receives five pitches (major league average), so that's 3,500 pitches over the course of the season. Each pitch, from the time it leaves the pitcher's hand until it reaches home plate, takes about one second. Therefore, 3,500 pitches take 3,500 seconds. Now if in 40 out of those 3,500 seconds, Jose Canseco does what he's paid to do — hit 40 home runs — he earns his $4.7 million. His entire season, therefore, from a results standpoint, takes just 40 seconds. The rest of the time and effort he puts in is just "stuff."

Now let's apply this same logic to your work as a life insurance agent:

• **Recognize that regardless of how much time and effort you put into your work, you get paid only for results.**

If you were to analyze all your insurance sale "home runs" over the past 12 months, the 10 minutes here when you said the right thing, the 15 minutes there when you made the right decision, the total time required for all these crucial results wouldn't add up to 24 hours. The rest of your activity — 1,500 to 2,000 hours of time and effort activity — was just "stuff."

In the course of the last year then, you were paid incredibly well for what you did in one day and nothing at all for the rest of your time. Since you weren't paid, why did you work?

Probably a good 1,000 hours of your "stuff" activity, if you hadn't done it all, wouldn't have made the least bit of difference as far as your results were concerned.

As a matter of fact, if you had taken those 1,000 hours as vacation (approximately 125 days), your results would have been even better, and much more enjoyable!

Strategy 16

RESULTS

• The biggest results in the world take only a few seconds or minutes.

Any agent who has put in 10 years in the business has developed a notion of how long his or her "results" take.

For example, we often hear agents who write big cases say: "Oh, those big cases, they can take 18 months to settle." Now the human brain is a very literal piece of equipment, so that when you say something takes 18 months, your brain will make sure it doesn't take any less time. But it doesn't take 18 months to settle! All of the crucial decisions required for settling the biggest life insurance policy in the world take only about a half hour; the rest of the process is just "stuff."

The results take only a few seconds or minutes. It's the **"not getting the results"** that takes the weeks, months, and years of time and effort.

Only a very few agents have learned how to focus just on the results, the home runs, in their work, and delegate all of the "stuff," all of the time and effort activities, to other people.

• Focus all support staff time and effort on achieving your most important results.

Your brain will do whatever you instruct it to do. That being the case, why not, as an insurance agent, instruct your brain to focus all your time, attention, expertise, and energy on just those few activities that actually produce the results? Take all the other activities and delegate them to members of your support team, training them on how they can focus their best efforts to support your results.

The agents that we have seen commit themselves to this process have found that their incomes doubled while the amount of time they actually worked was halved. They forever leave behind the time and effort world of the lower-producing and chronically frustrated life insurance agents who think that it takes a long time to achieve results.

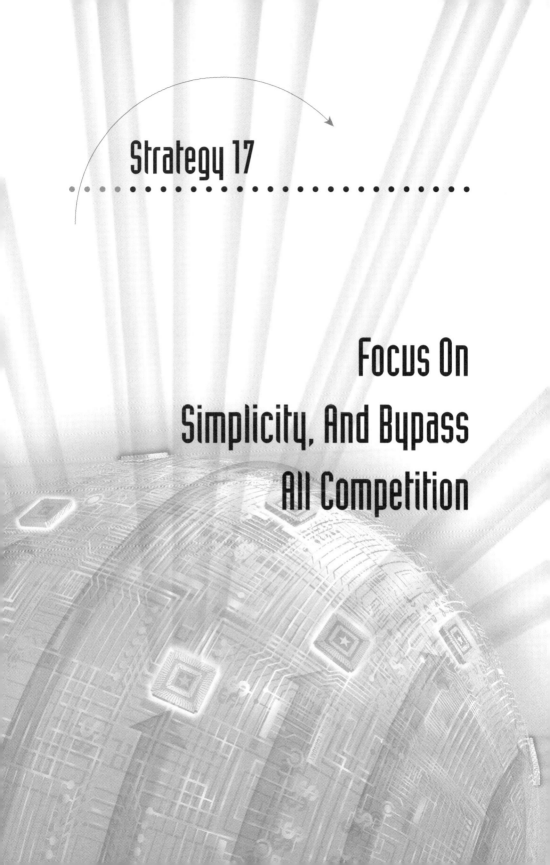

Strategy 17

Focus On Simplicity, And Bypass All Competition

Strategy 17

Focus On Simplicity, And Bypass All Competition

As all bureaucracies, including those in the insurance industry, continue to collapse as a result of microtechnology, most people's working lives will become very complicated: filled with confusion, conflicts, and complexity. And all because they will be bombarded with far too much information for the human brain to process usefully.

Therefore, the losers in today's world are those who feel threatened by change, who feel that they are falling behind, and who feel that something that is out of their control can happen at any moment to make their jobs superfluous and their lives more difficult.

If these are losers, then it's easy to see who will be the winners — those who can establish and maintain the simplest approach to their personal and business lives over long periods of time.

This "simplest approach to life" means basing one's decisions and actions on a system of strategic principles which do not have to be changed or replaced for the remainder of one's life.

The 21ˢᵗ Century Agent will create his or her insurance practice on a foundation of personal knowledge that ignores the complexities, conflicts, and complications of the collapsing bureaucratic world.

One of the greatest skills of the 21ˢᵗ century, therefore, will be the ability to *ignore* vast amounts of information. The key to success in the "information revolution" or "knowledge economy," paradoxically, will not be in how much one knows, but rather in how little one needs to know.

In fact, over the next 25 years, a completely successful personal and business life can be built on mastering just the following seven areas of personal knowledge:

• Knowledge of how to stay healthy, fit, and energetic until you are 100 years old.

All of the information needed to accomplish this is available in a dozen different books at any book store, or from a skilled fitness consultant at any good health club or spa. All you need to do is read the book, sign up with the consultant, and establish a good routine of nutrition, sleep, and exercise. Then make this routine the daily foundation of your lifestyle for the rest of your life. As the commercial says, just do it.

• Knowledge of how to make, save, and manage enough money for lifetime security.

No mystery here, just follow the same advice that you have been selling to others for the past five, 10, 20, or 50 years. Only, as was suggested in Strategy 15, put yourself under the coaching and management of a skilled financial consultant. As far as making money goes, you're already in an excellent industry for doing that over the next 25 years.

• Knowledge of how to manage your time for the purpose of personal achievement and satisfaction.

Aside from your three most important money-making activities (Strategy 12), there isn't anything else you should be doing when you are working. When you're not working, focus your time on all of the other dimensions of your life (Strategy 1). Work strategically, play superbly.

Strategy 17

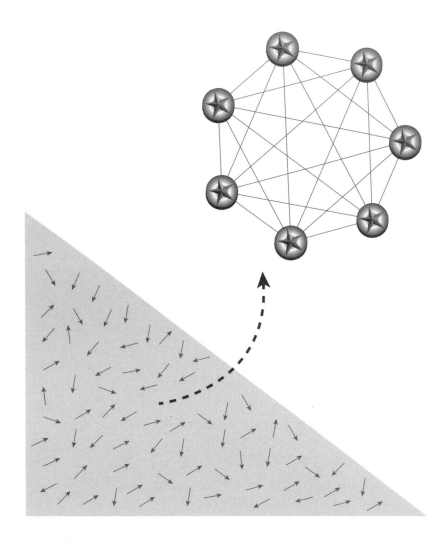

- **Knowledge of how to be referable to the people who can provide the biggest opportunities.**

This will be covered more fully in Strategy 18, but there's a simple rule provided to us by David Cowper, one of the first Top of the Table agents we worked with in the 1970s: "If you would sell what John Smith buys, you must see through John Smith's eyes." Referability is the simple result of seeing the world as other people see it, and adding value to the things that are important to them.

- **Knowledge of how to establish, cultivate, and maintain life-time relationships with the people you love.**

Rule Number 1: love them. Rules 2 to 100: see Rule Number 1. At the base of all love there is first of all showing respect for the other person's uniqueness, and then secondly, expressing appreciation for how that uniqueness affects you. If you respect and appreciate the people you love on a daily basis, you will have a lifetime relationship with them. Guaranteed.

- **Knowledge of how to identify, focus, and reinforce your unique ability in life.**

Everyone has a unique ability, but only a few ever get clear about it in the course of their lives — mainly because they try to be all things to all people. Review Strategies 12 and 14 again.

- **Knowledge of how to transform your unique ability into genius-level performance and results.**

If you focus all of your energies on your three most important focus activities for the next 10 years, at the end of those 10 years you will begin thinking, speaking, and acting like a genius.

Did we miss any important information? If you master these seven areas of knowledge, will the "knowledge economy" leave you behind? Not likely. In fact, you will be such a shining beacon of calmness, clarity, and confidence that hundreds and thousands of others will pay just for the opportunity to organize their lives on your example.

Strategy 18

Focus On Referability, And Multiply Personal Confidence

Strategy 18

In order to achieve high results in the best markets, agents have to be highly referable. Many agents fail in this respect, and lack personal confidence because they have neglected to develop the following four crucial "referability habits" in their professional development:

- *Show up on time*
- *Do what they say*
- *Finish what they start*
- *Say please and thank you*

Anyone who fails to do these four things on a consistent basis will find it difficult to be referred regardless of how talented a salesperson or how brilliant an insurance technician he or she may be.

The 21st Century Agent will build his or her entire career on these four referability habits, thereby achieving ever greater personal confidence, and even bigger sales opportunities.

These seem like common sense, don't they. This is kid's stuff. Surely there must be more to being referred than this, isn't there? What about a sense of humor, super intelligence, and good looks? All of these can add to one's referability in the marketplace, but if the four habits listed above are missing, then none of these other qualities will do you much good over the long run.

There are a lot of funny, brilliant, good-looking individuals who can't get anywhere as insurance agents because they think they're too good to practice the four referability habits.

Here's why the habits are so important:

Each of these habits is based on showing respect and appreciation for other people. Every person you meet is the center of his or her own universe. When you demonstrate from the very beginning of a relationship — through your consistent, habitual behavior — that you recognize the central importance of the other person's schedule, commitments, deadlines, and goals, you immediately become an invaluable resource in that other person's life. He or she will want to refer you into other important relationships and situations.

But there are also a lot of life insurance agents who have never quite grasped why referrals are so important. They display almost a lackadaisical and flippant attitude towards the whole process of obtaining and utilizing referrals — perhaps thinking that they can make it big by doing cold calls all their life.

Whatever the reason, they deprive themselves of the single biggest marketing resource that any entrepreneur can have in the marketplace — dozens and hundreds of influential clients and customers recommending them to their friends, colleagues, and peers.

In order to master this process, several important points need to be grasped:

• Recognize that high quality referrals are the most powerful form of marketing.

Michael Jordan makes $25 million a year doing commercials, because McDonald's and Nike, to name two advertisers who use him, think that his recommendation of their product is worth a lot of money to them. If Michael Jordan thinks a Big Mac is great, then so will millions of TV viewers. If he thinks that Nikes are neat shoes to wear, then

Strategy 18

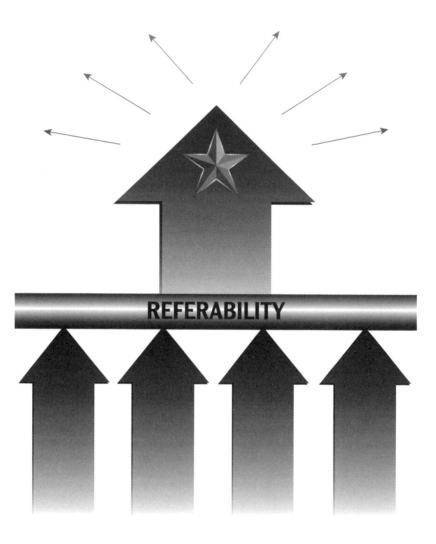

so will millions of his fans. If star athletes and entertainers like Michael Jordan get paid for their recommendations and people still believe them, then what about someone recommending you for free?

• **Recognize that your 20 best clients right now can be an unlimited referral network.**

In a conversation several years ago with a successful agent, we asked him what the combined net worth was of his 20 best clients. After thinking about it, he guessed that it was approximately $250 million.

Then we asked him to think about this possibility — if his 20 best clients were to provide 20 referrals to their best relationships, in other words 20 x 20 = 400, what would the combined net worth be of those additional 400 high quality prospects? He guessed that it would be in the neighborhood of $3 billion.

Finally, we asked him what his income goal was for that year. He said $800,000. "Well," we told him, "in a group worth $3 billion, all you have to do is check the sofas after they stand up, and you'll find $800,000!"

If you use your 20 best clients as a referral network, they can introduce you to unlimited opportunities.

• **In a world of unreliable people, the four referability habits will make you a prized resource.**

What do people want in return for referring you into high quality situations? Surprisingly little, except the assurance that they're not going to be sorry for doing it. Because the world is changing rapidly right now, a lot of people, including many insurance agents, are unreliable when it comes to the four referability habits.

They *don't* show up on time.

They *don't* do what they say.

They *don't* finish what they start.

And *they* don't say please and thank you.

On the other hand, when people come across someone who is good at these four habits, they talk about him or her as a prized resource to everybody they know.

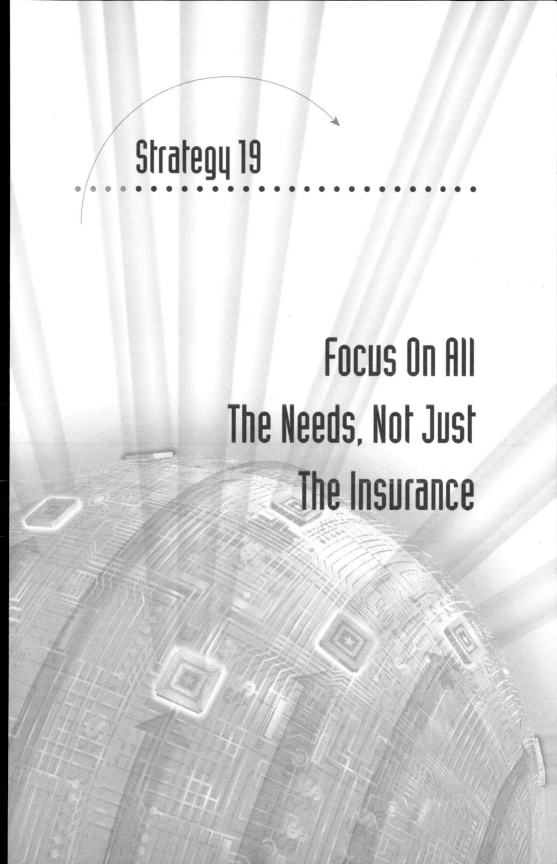

Strategy 19

Focus On All The Needs, Not Just The Insurance

Strategy 19

Focus On All The Needs, Not Just The Insurance

There's an old Arab saying: "When a pickpocket looks at a saint, all he sees are pockets." This points out a natural tendency of most people to see things entirely from their own viewpoint. But that's not how you make sales, regardless of what you are selling.

Agents may look at the world from the standpoint of life insurance, but prospects and clients very definitely do not. The latter see their future in terms of dreams, aspirations, desires, and goals as well as problems, obstacles, crises, and deficiencies.

Therefore, in order to make big life insurance sales, life insurance agents have to stop looking for the life insurance sale, and start looking for the fundamental needs that need solutions.

This will ensure that the insurance solution will be an integrated part of the client's overall approach to the future. It will also insure that once the insurance is sold, it will stay sold.

The 21st Century Agent will become a total counselor to his or her clients, not just a seller of insurance products. In doing so, the agent will become a lifelong supporter of the client's total growth and achievement.

One of the reasons why effective salespeople in all fields are highly paid is because so few human beings seem to have the salesperson's creative ability to see the world through another person's eyes.

Most people want to get other people to see things according to their needs. The effective salesperson goes in an opposite direction — he or she wants to see things according to the other person's needs.

Essentially, selling is the activity of aligning specific resources with specific needs to create specific solutions and then getting paid for it.

This is easy to understand, and it's also easy to accomplish, if you keep the following points in mind:

• Think in terms of the client's future, without reference to your own.

The greatest entertainers are those who can experience the performance totally from the audience's point of view. The greatest life insurance agents are those who can experience the future entirely from the client's point of view.

For most agents, suspending self-interest is a difficult if not impossible thing to do. For the vast majority of agents, selling means survival. The average income for agents in North America is somewhere around $35,000, which doesn't buy very much confidence in today's economy.

It's hard to give very much attention to someone else's future when you're preoccupied with your own. When your next sale is directly related to your next month's mortgage payment, there's a tendency to want a quick sale that will settle fast. The client will sense that you are not interested in his or her needs, and will resist the selling process.

But if you reverse this thinking, and ignore your own needs, then it becomes possible to enter a dimension where the client is a partner in the selling process. He or she will sense that you are totally focused on his or her needs and, confident about this, will do everything possible to assist you in creating the biggest and best possible solution.

Strategy 19

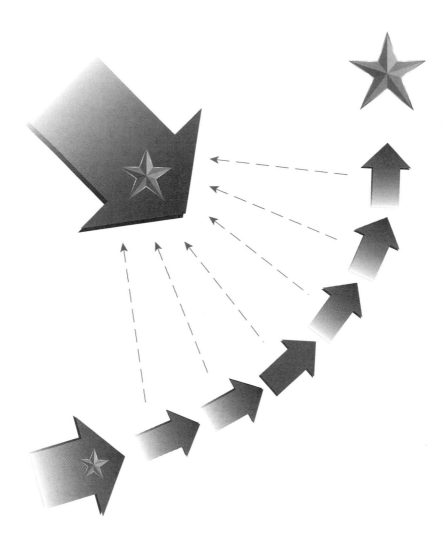

• **Remember that you don't even have a product until the client has a gameplan.**

Life insurance companies talk about their "products" all the time because many head office bureaucrats still think they're running a factory — convinced that they are involved in a mass production, mass marketing, and mass distribution industry.

Probably because of this head office mentality, there's a tendency among insurance agents to talk about their "product," when in fact they don't really have a product.

Life insurance as a product does not even come into existence until there is a creative synthesis involving an agent's experience and expertise on the one hand, and a client's gameplan for the future on the other. It must exist as a reality in the creative imagination of the agent and the client before it can exist as an economic reality in the asset base of an insurance company.

• **Guide the client to "map the future" in terms of the most important needs and solutions.**

Most people have images in their minds about how they would like their future to unfold. But these images tend to be vague and incoherent until someone asks a series of questions that helps to clarify the images, organize them, and give them an overall structure and direction.

That's what you as an agent can do for your clients. By first asking the three-year question in Strategy 9, and then a series of follow-up questions to clarify the person's specific needs and goals, a life insurance agent can become a client's most useful advisor over a period of many years.

Helping successful people to become clearer about their future and excited about their prospects is perhaps the greatest service that we can provide to anyone, but it's not simply an altruistic exercise. The answers you get invariably open the door to large insurance sales. And surrounding yourself with people with exciting futures creates a motivating environment that helps you to achieve your own goals.

Strategy 20

Focus On The Global Economy, And Reinterpret The Insurance Industry

Strategy 20

At one time there were strict regulatory barriers separating the four main financial industries: banking, insurance, investments, and trusts. But with the advent of microtechnology, these barriers have been crumbling so that banks now sell insurance, investment brokers provide banking, and insurance agents sell investments.

Over the next 25 years, a single global financial services industry will emerge, in which banking, insurance, investments and trusts are just different names for thousands of kinds of financial products that will be sold and purchased as commodities.

The 21st Century Agent, as an entrepreneur, will pay attention to the continually evolving global economy and utilize insurance as one of many solutions for satisfying client needs and requirements.

For the past 125 years, the most useful information a life insurance agent could receive throughout his or her career came from the insurance companies. They had the experience, research, and expertise to tell the agent where the industry was going over the next 25 years. Around 1975, all that changed when the use of microtechnology began to pull down the barriers between life insurance and all other financial industries.

From the standpoint of consumers, life insurance became just one kind of economic strategy, and life insurance agents became just one kind of economic player. It was now a global game, and the life insurance companies could no longer predict how the game was going to be played over the course of an agent's career.

Twenty years later, microchips are 4,000 times faster, the global financial services game has speeded up by the same factor, and the head offices of many insurance companies, still mired in bureaucratic processes, are out of touch. They must now rely increasingly on the agents in the field to tell them where the industry is going.

That's why agents should start using the global economy itself as their main source of knowledge, and for the most part take insurance company predictions and strategies as just so much information, most of it useless, before it hits the streets.

The question to be answered then is: What is the global economy telling us? Several things:

• In all industries, the consumers, not the manufacturers, are now calling the shots.

What is happening in the life insurance industry right now is the same thing that happened in the retail industry when bar coding was introduced in the 1970s. The manufacturers had all the research, and the retailers had none.

Before bar coding, manufacturers dictated terms to retailers — how products were to be marketed, how much product was to be purchased, when it was to be paid for, and at what price it was to be sold. After bar coding, retailers knew at the end of each sales day how much product had been sold and what pricing strategies were needed for the next day. Having this information, they began to dictate terms to the manufacturers.

Armed with computer technology, sophisticated software, and global communication link-ups, life insurance agents over the next 25 years will increasingly dictate terms to the life insurance companies.

Strategy 20

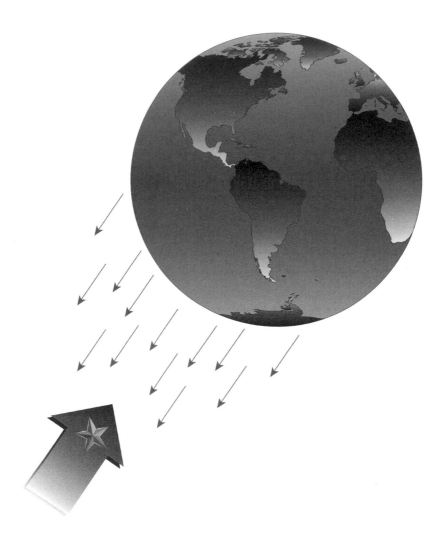

Agents are in daily communication with consumers — life insurance companies are not.

• Knowledge is now more valuable than capital, equipment, and personnel.

A strange reality results from microtechnology — the information about things is now more valuable than the things themselves.

One example is airline reservation systems. If you take the market value of all the airline reservation systems, they are worth more than the airlines.

Another example: TV Guide. If you take the market value of all the local editions of TV Guide, they are worth more than all the television networks.

A third example: Bill Gates. If the man and his ideas leave Microsoft today, the company's stock drops by 25% tomorrow.

Bringing this back to you — the collective marketing knowledge of the top 10,000 life insurance agents is worth more than the capital, equipment, and head office personnel of all the life insurance companies.

• Human creativity is overwhelming human conformity.

Everywhere you look today, systems based on conformity are giving way to systems based on creative choice.

This is why the Soviet Union collapsed, this is why the vaunted Japanese manufacturing economy has hit a stone wall, and this is why bureaucratic organizations everywhere are falling apart.

Microtechnology has now created the possibility for every person on the planet to be an expert on his or her own future. It may take another century before this is a reality for more than a small percentage of the population, but the global trend is irreversibly in the direction of greater individual autonomy.

During the 21ˢᵗ century, the key players in this entire process, in every industry, will be the "agents" — those who are able to bring just the right knowledge to just the right people at just the right time.

Summary

Think Of The Next 25 Years As A Single Strategy

Summary

Think Of The Next 25 Years As A Single Strategy

If you had been born somewhere in central Europe in 1455, the world around you would have been much the same as it had been for the previous 500 years. Everywhere you looked, daily life was controlled by a vast web of rules and structures created by religious authorities. The rules were frequently inhumane, the structures oppressive, and the authorities arrogant and corrupt, but hardly anyone noticed because this is the way that things had always been done.

Yet in that same year of 1455, Gutenburg invented movable type, and over the next 100 years the political power of religious authorities was effectively destroyed throughout Europe as millions of individuals gained access to new kinds of knowledge in newspapers, pamphlets, and books.

The world began the great crossover from religion, as the central organizing structure, to politics and the emergence of the great nation states.

In 1970, more than 500 years after Gutenburg's invention, the world was organized on the basis of huge bureaucratic structures — national governments, corporations, and unions. Everywhere you looked, people lived their lives based on bureaucratic rules, regulations, and expectations. The rules were frequently rigid, the regulations restrictive, and the expectations limiting and uncreative. But hardly anyone noticed because this is the way things had been done for more than 70 years.

Bureaucracy was the way things had been organized throughout the 20ᵗʰ century, and all the experts on organization in the 1950s predicted that every aspect of human life would fall under the greater control of bureaucratic authorities by the year 2000.

Yet 25 years later, nobody believes that anymore. The rapid proliferation of microtechnology has enabled hundreds of millions, and soon billions, of human beings to gain access to new kinds of knowledge through computers, satellite and cable TV, facsimile machines, desktop publishing, wireless phones, and the vast network of data networks known as the Internet.

And so the world has now begun another great crossover — this time from politics, as the central organizing structure, to economics and the emergence of the global economic system.

Over the next 25 years, much of what people took for granted during the great bureaucratic age of the 20ᵗʰ century is going to be turned on its head. Nowhere will this be more true than in the life insurance industry, where some of the great bureaucracies have expanded continually since the mid-1800s.

All of this is going to come to an end, and quite suddenly. Entirely new kinds of organizational structures and alliances based on microchip networks are going to replace the head office pyramids.

There will be four separate groups of individuals who will survive this upheaval: the entrepreneurial executives, the entrepreneurial brokerage managers, the producer groups, and the entrepreneurial agents.

• **The Entrepreneurial Executives: superb asset managers and service providers.**

Among the thousands of bureaucratic executives at the senior levels of insurance companies, there is a small but growing number of skilled, enthusiastic, and ambitious individuals who have no vested interest in perpetuating the bureaucratic regimes. If it were up to them, the companies would be radically smaller, more automated, more consumer-driven, and taking far greater advantage of the entrepreneurial knowledge and capabilities of independent agents.

Over the next quarter century, these entrepreneurial executives are going to gain control of the companies, as the bureaucrats can no longer cope with the challenges of the global economy.

• **The Entrepreneurial Brokerage Managers: superb facilitators of independent high producers.**

The career agency system, as it has traditionally existed, is dead, dying, or beginning the process of decline. A few systems may survive indefinitely, but each year fewer agents will be recruited, and fewer lives written.

Many managers and general agents in these systems who have been bureaucratic in their outlook will not survive the collapse; but a new class of entrepreneurial life insurance managers is emerging from the debris of the old agency structures. They are experts at organizing and expanding networks of independent agents, and they facilitate the growth of high producers. This concept is called the *brokerage agency network,* an example being the Advanced Insurance Network, a nationwide organization of experienced general agents, operating as entrepreneurs, who provide a full range of products and services from several companies to thousands of independent agents.

• **The Entrepreneurial Producer Groups: superb integrators of the best agents and the best companies.**

The producer groups will become to the life insurance industry what the price clubs have become to the retail industry. Hundreds, perhaps thousands of entrepreneurial agents will combine their marketing and negotiating power within a single collective. There will probably be hundreds of these collectives by 2020, all held together and able to expand because of powerful software and communications technologies. Some producer groups will develop their own re-insurance capabilities to support the special case underwriting of their members. The different groups will compete for the best agents in the same way that universities in the U.S. compete for the best high school athletes. And the entrepreneurial insurance companies will compete for the business of the best producer groups.

• The Entrepreneurial Agents: superb problem solvers for clients with big futures.

On the previous pages, we have outlined the prospects, ground rules, and direction for the approximately 20,000 or so entrepreneurial agents who are going to be the real catalysts in the 21ˢᵗ century life insurance industry. The secret to their success — the secret to your success as a 21ˢᵗ Century Agent — is really no secret at all. All the trends and strategies listed in this book represent information given to us over the past 20 years by more than 500 top agents who have participated in The Strategic Coach Program. Each one of them had a piece of the puzzle, but because all of them lead busy lives, no one had taken the time to put the whole puzzle together.

The 21ˢᵗ Century Agent, therefore, integrates everything that these 500 agents have contributed into a single strategic system that an entrepreneurial agent can use to grow and thrive in the global economy of the next 25 years.

Acknowledgments

Acknowledgments

Over the past 20 years, we have had both the advantage and the privilege of consulting with and coaching over 500 highly successful life insurance agents, more than 300 of whom are current clients in The Strategic Coach Program. In writing this book, it became apparent that we have learned as much from these individuals as they have from us.

In particular there are a number of agents who became for us the role models for The 21st Century Agent, who in fact provided us with the picture of the future that we translated into the trends and strategies on the previous pages.

This group includes David Cowper, Gord Berger, Frank Creaghan, Joe Pal, Paul Goldstein, Ted Snider, Peter Creaghan, and Marty McConnell.

In addition, there have been countless hours of discussion over the years with other agents, managers, executives, and consultants, whose insights and observations were invaluable in fashioning the overall concept of The 21st Century Agent:

Mary Lou Gutscher, Mary Lou Taylor, Ted Polci, Ted Warburton, Don Drinkwalter, David Ryckman, Sid Friedman, Jack Bradley, Bob Bensman, Dermot Healey, Phil Howe, Rob Crowder, Elizabeth Bowden,

Tom Lytle, Pat Barry, Ken Wilton, Judy Byle-Jones, Irene Bailey, Bruce Etherington, Todd Healy, Jim Milonas, Gary Wright, Sonny Goldstein, Gerry Sacks, Charles Melvin, Ray Silva, Larry Kinlin, Ed Jamieson, Bob Hamilton, Harry Schiavone, Joe Himelick, Desmond Kidd, Dan Conlin, Lee Warner, Bob Carter, Kelly Kidd, Stan Parke, Bob Adams, Rick Thorpe, Norm Gilbert, Teri Bergstrom, Lou Cassara, Tommy Ingram, John Williams, Mike Toomey, Stanley Thal, Lee Canfield, John Balis, Joe Stone, Allan Oxman, John Backhouse, Malcolm Doney, Tracy Sunderlage, Joel Shapiro, Stan Lang, David Forest, Hugh Arison, Mark Echlin, Ross Gilchrist, Paul Bourbonniere, Murray Morton, Fraser Deacon, Greg Deacon, Kirk Polson, Sandy Schmidt, Tom Olexa, Wayne Cotton, John Firstbrook, Dennis Caponi, Tom Hazel, Raymond Matt, Leonard Vis, Steve Pascal, Don Smith, Eugene Eberley, Gene Emery, Nancy Franklin, Nicole Sung, Bill Dyer, Roger Fox, Aurele Campeau, Leonard Klassen, Doug Atkinson, Bill Bell, Raynor McCullough, Les Trelenberg, Gerard Arsenault, Louis Bamberg, Lee Churchill, Malcolm Doney, David Forest, Jacques Gibbs, John Iacobelli, Jim Jones, Michael Kaleel, Leon Levy, Mac Lowry, Bill O'Donnell, Michael Rosenzweig, Manny Sarris, Sanford Schmidt, Jeff Warren, Bob Warther, Tim Shoecraft, Lowen Rosenthal, Gary Sitzmann, Gregory Acosta, John Behr, Tom Cohn, Stan Ellis, Nancy Hogarth, Robert Mundy, Roland Nebeker, Lloyd Wilson, Seymour Cohen, John Baird, Verne Smith, Alan Maltenfort, Pat Collins, Jamie Garard, Charlie Walsh, John Burton, and Garnet Morris.

There are a number of other individuals with whom we have spoken over the past two decades who have provided valuable information and advice. To these and all of the above, we express our deepest appreciation.

Last but not least, my deepest thanks to Babs Smith, my wife, my partner, and the guiding genius of the company; our great production team: Sonja Moser, Sean Tamblyn, Ross Slater, Steve Pecile, Sonja Persram, Shannon Waller, Reinhold Schieber, Marni Andrews, and Andy Cameron; our fabulous team at The Strategic Coach Inc., and all past and present participants of The Strategic Coach Program.

About
The Author

About The Author

Dan Sullivan is co-founder and president of The Strategic Coach Inc., which provides a lifetime focusing program for highly successful entrepreneurs throughout North America.

At present, more than 1000 entrepreneurs in 60 different industries are utilizing The Strategic Coach Program to simplify their work lives, increase their income and savings, and enhance the quality of their personal lives.

Among the current Strategic Coach clients are 300 MDRT agents and more than 50 who achieved Top of the Table in 1994.

Before coming to Canada in 1971, Dan Sullivan attended Catholic University in Washington, D.C. and graduated from St. John's College in Annapolis, Maryland, an institution renowned for its Great Books Program. During the Vietnam conflict, he served from 1965–67 as entertainment coordinator with the Eighth U.S. Army in South Korea. He has extensive experience in the areas of theatre and journalism and was a writer with Baker, Lovick Advertising in Toronto from 1971 to 1974.

Mr. Sullivan is married to Babs Smith, and they jointly own and operate The Strategic Coach in Chicago and Toronto.

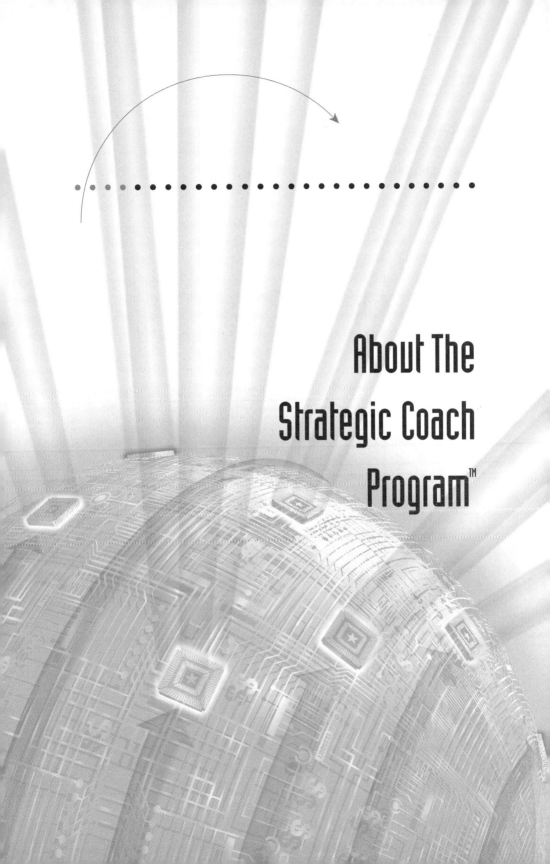

About The
Strategic Coach
Program™

The Strategic Coach Program™

The concepts and strategies in this book have been developed over the past 10 years within the context of The Strategic Coach Program.

The Program is a three-year focusing school for experienced and successful entrepreneurs, with participants from throughout North America and abroad.

The Strategic Coach is designed for three purposes:

1. To eliminate from an entrepreneur's life all the "stuff" and "messes" that interfere with productivity.

2. To increase the entrepreneur's concentration on the most important money-making relationships and centers of influence.

3. To increase dramatically the amount of free time that can be devoted to personal relationships, increased health, etc. — all the personal interests that make being an entrepreneur worthwhile.

The Strategic Coach is a system.

The Program consists of 12 fundamental "breakthrough strategies," mastered over a period of three years, that systematically simplify and clarify everything that the entrepreneur thinks, says, plans, and does.

These 12 strategies, when implemented and integrated with each other, create a permanent condition of high energy and creativity in which the entrepreneur's resources are focused entirely on the most important opportunities.

The Strategic Coach is a philosophy, a structure, a process, and a methodology.

The Program lasts three years, which is sufficient time to establish and change fundamental entrepreneurial habits. Over that period there are 12 one-day workshops at 90-day intervals, each of which enables entrepreneurs, in the company of other entrepreneurs, to achieve a deeper understanding of the 12 focusing strategies.

Entrepreneurs who enroll in The Strategic Coach have come to a point in their careers when the skills, experience, and opportunity are there, and it is time to put everything together. What is needed for further progress — for their next quantum leap — is a clear-cut statement of vision, a strategic gameplan for taking action, a structure to keep them on track, a team of other high performers to keep them honest, and an experienced coach to keep them focused.

If you would like further information about The Strategic Coach Program, and other Strategic Coach services and products, please telephone 416·531·7399 or 1·800·387·3206.

Suggested Further Reading

Suggested Further Reading

Although these books do not represent a basis or framework for The 21st Century Agent™, they will help reinforce new thinking and a new focus for the future.

- *Built To Last.* James Collins, Jerry Porras: Harper Collins, 1994.

- *Unlimited Wealth.* Paul Zane Pilzer: Crown Publishing, 1990.

- *Post Capitalist Society.* Peter Drucker: Harper Collins, 1994

- *The Great Crossover: Personal Confidence In The Age Of The Microchip.* Dan Sullivan: The Strategic Coach Inc., 1994.

- *Death of Money.* Joel Kurtzmann: Little Brown, 1994.

- *Pure Instinct.* Kathy Kolbe: Random House (Times Books), 1993.

- *Technotrends.* Daniel Burrus: Harper Collins, 1994.

- *The Popcorn Report.* Faith Popcorn: Harper Collins, 1994.

- *The Age of Unreason.* Charles Handy: Harvard Business School Press, 1990

- *Shifting Gears.* Nuala Beck: Harper Collins, 1993.

- *Out of Control: The Rise of Neo-Biological Civilization.* Kevin Kelly: Addison-Wesley, 1994